Introduction

This Expert Toolkit Bundle is a compilation of 11 tools, methods, guides and frameworks targeted at anyone who wants to become a highly proficient strategic business advisor.

The contents of the bundle are by no means exhaustive, but they will provide a very solid platform to build upon for anyone moving along the path towards becoming an advisor to business's large and small. The included tools have stood the test of time, and the team at Expert Toolkit believes they will be powerful and value-adding in the hands of the competent practitioner.

The bundle contains a diverse range of tools and techniques intended to build the core skills and knowledge necessary to be an effective advisor across key areas including financial, market, competition, business strategy, operating model and business mergers.

We hope you find the contents of this bundle useful. Please contact us if you have any questions or feedback, or if we can help you craft a tailored training or delivery program for your organization.

the team @ Expert Toolkit

Contents of this Expert Toolkit Bundle

1. Essentials of Operating Model Design

2. Guide to Financial Ratio Analysis

3. Mastering Market Sizing and Share Analysis

4. Introduction to Post-Merger Integration

5. Essentials of Porter's Five Forces

6. Introduction to PEST Analysis

7. Mastering SWOT Analysis

8. Mastering Competition Analysis

9. Guide to Hypothesis-based Analysis

10. How to use the Accelerated SWOT Method

11. Accelerated SWOT Method Template

Operating Model Essentials

Learn the fundamental principles and components of Operating Models and how they can help describe and transform a business

> "All men can see these tactics whereby I conquer, but what none can see is the strategy out of which victory is evolved."
>
> *Sun Tzu*

Objectives of this Expert Toolkit Guide

1. Provide a foundational understanding of Operating Models and how they can deliver value in a business context

2. Outline the different types of Operating Models and how they can be utilized to improve business performance

3. Provide proven practices, principles and steps for developing a good Future State Operating Model

4. Provide examples of different types of Operating Models to help increase understanding

What is an operating model?

As the name implies, an Operating Model describes how an organization operates – as an integrated whole consisting of many parts.

- It represents a single view of the organization across people, process and technology.

- It focuses on what is important to the organization.

- It describes either how the organization works today (As-Is) or how it wishes to operate in the future (To-Be).

- Together, the As-Is and To-Be Models can be the foundation for organizations that want to transform.

- A Future State (or To-Be) Operating Model takes into consideration the relevant business drivers (internal and external) and business strategy, objectives and vision.

- Operating Models need to consider a range of elements that must be understood and incorporated to make the entire "system" operate in an integrated and coordinated manner.

Typical elements needed to make the organization work:

- Customers, Segments & Channels
- Business Units
- Services & Products
- Processes
- Technology Systems
- People & Structure
- Physical Infrastructure

The aim of an operating model is to describe how each business element relates to each other to deliver a specific objective or set of objectives.

What is an operating model?

It Describes the Who and the How Behind the What and the Why

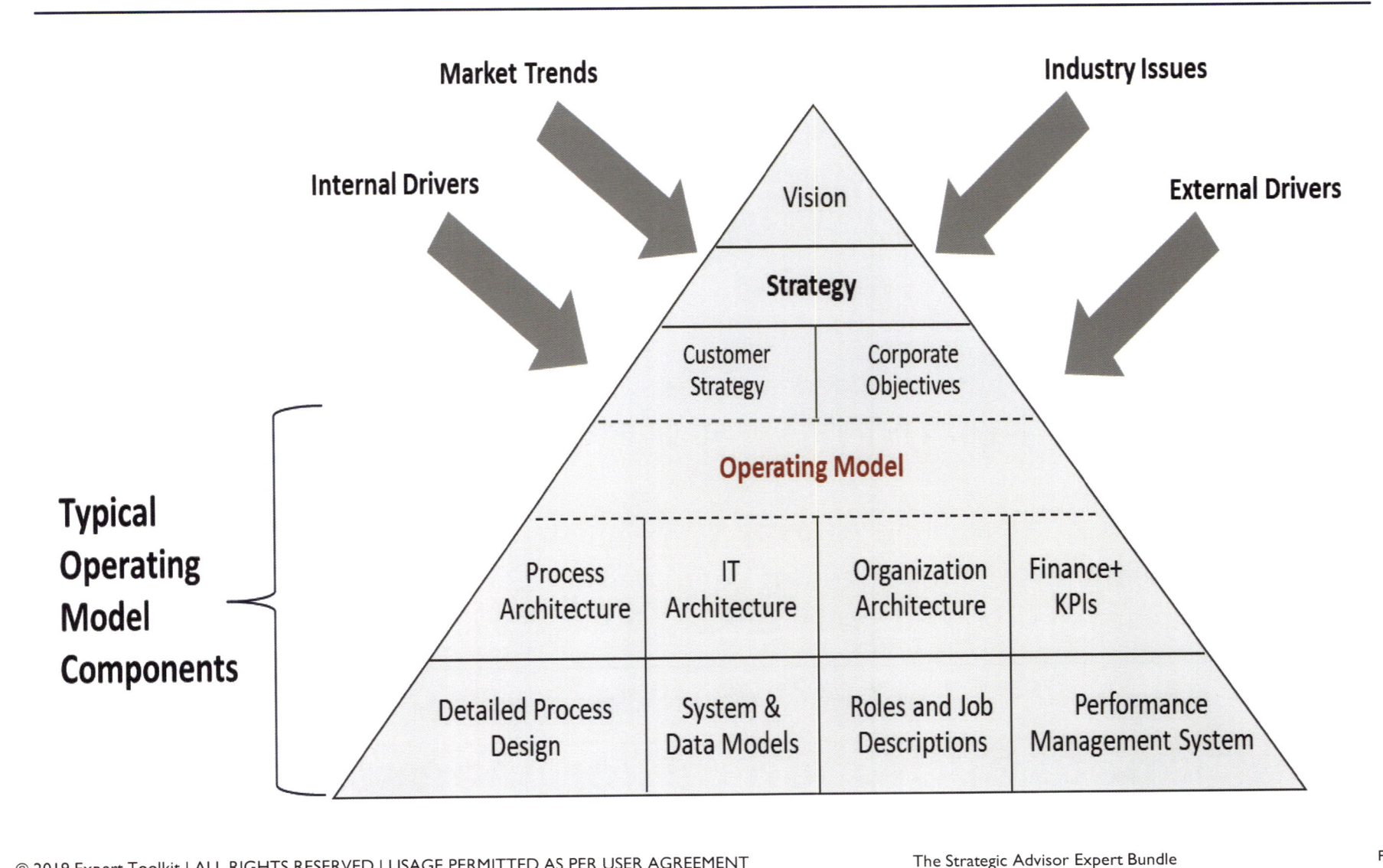

Market Trends →

Industry Issues →

Internal Drivers →

External Drivers →

Pyramid diagram:
- Top: Vision
- **Strategy**: Customer Strategy | Corporate Objectives
- **Operating Model**:
  - Process Architecture | IT Architecture | Organization Architecture | Finance+ KPIs
  - Detailed Process Design | System & Data Models | Roles and Job Descriptions | Performance Management System

Typical Operating Model Components (brackets the lower portion of the pyramid)

The business need for an operating model

What Value Does an Operating Model Bring to a Business?

- An operating model describes the way that a business structures its capabilities to execute its strategies. It is not unusual that a company employs multiple operating models to represent different business units or other dimensions (geographic, product, subsidiary, etc.).

- An operating model shows what capabilities are needed to form an end-to-end strategic value chain, and who and where the capabilities are to be performed.

- An operating model includes how each capability is arranged to drive maximum efficiency and effectiveness.

- The construction of an operating model begins with a business strategy that incorporates deliberate decisions about customers, products, routes-to-market and value capture methods. The business strategy is typically defined in terms of agreed business segments, markets and customers that serve as the targets for execution of an operating model.

- A good, effective operating model should incorporate all of the key elements necessary to describe how a business is being organized to accomplish its aims.

Why are operating models important?

They Provide the Big Picture
An organization's operating model can provide a clear, 'big picture' outline of what the organization does and how it does it. It describes – in a single view – how the various components of the organization come together to work as a whole.

They Facilitate Strategic Choices
When considering new strategies or the impact of market forces, an operating model will assist in evaluating options and impacts. Should major change be required, operating model re-design will help accomplish optimized outcomes.

They Link Strategy to Execution
An operating model takes a business strategy (that typically describes "what" and "for who" in addition to the "why") and puts it into more detail with the aid of graphical representation and the aim of describing the "how".

They Guide Transformation
A clear future state Operating Model provides a sound framework for describing an end state which can then guide necessary transformational change. This change comes about by through the evolution that is needed going from the As-Is to the To-Be.

The different types of operating models

An Operating Model is generally developed in order to describe the current state in a holistic fashion or to support the design, planning and implementation of a future state way of operating. This future state is typically associated with a set of understood business drivers and agreed strategic objectives.

Often a current state operating model and future state operating model will work together to outline a need for change. There are two primary ways to present an Operating Model:

- **High Level Operating Model**

    - Useful for developing strategic options and facilitating discussions with senior stakeholders.

- **Detailed Operating Model**

    - Useful for integrating detailed people, process and technology analysis with financial modelling.

	Now	Future
High Level	High Level Current State(or As-Is) Operating Model	High Level Target (or Future State, To-Be) Operating Model
Detailed	Detailed Current State (or As-Is) Operating Model	Detailed Target (or Future State, To-Be) Operating Model

The above models can be used together to describe the same set of circumstances to a different level of detail – from strategy to design and operational execution

The value of a current state or as-is model

A Clear As-Is Operating Model is the Basis for Any Change

An As-Is Operating Model facilitates understanding amongst stakeholders and does this by doing the following:

- Scoping, structuring and clarifying the current operating model;
- Describing the activities and services that a business currently performs;
- Describing all services, functions or processes that the organization delivers;
- Aiding in performance-diagnosis and gap analysis on the current operating model;
- Aiding the assessment of performance across customer, market and financial perspectives.
- To find out what are the causes of underperformance with the organization

	Now	Future
High Level	High Level Current State (or As-Is) Operating Model	High Level Target (or Future State, To-Be) Operating Model
Detailed	Detailed Current State (or As-Is) Operating Model	Detailed Target (or Future State, To-Be) Operating Model

An As-Is Operating Model provides a good basis of understanding to build upon a case for transformation change to a future state operating model

Operating models facilitate transformation

Operating Models Support Crafting Clear and Structured Change Agendas

Common Issues with Transformation	How Operating Models Help
• Describing a large, complex organization clearly to lead and evolve it effectively	• Provides a clear view of the organization at all levels and describes how each part inter-relates and influences the attainment of the strategy
• Understanding and communicating the root causes of performance issues within an organization	• Informs both goal setting, capability gaps, risks and transformation prioritization
• Describing the goals of a future organization that balances the delivery of value to both customers and shareholders	• Allows a transformation program to be compartmentalized into discrete components necessary to implement the new strategy
• Identifying the strategic options, and being able to select the most appropriate option in an objective, holistic manner	• Provides a structured approach for assessing strategic transformation options and choosing the optimal one
• Delivering transformation in an effective and efficient way in order to realize the benefits of an improved future state	• Facilitates transformation design and delivery across people, process and technology
• Understanding the dynamics, the needs and interconnectivity of an organization in order to manage its performance effectively	• Assists with the development of an effective performance management approach which is essential for transformation success and long term business excellence

© 2019 Expert Toolkit | ALL RIGHTS RESERVED | USAGE PERMITTED AS PER USER AGREEMENT   The Strategic Advisor Expert Bundle

Designing a Future State Operating Model

Future state design is a 5 step process

The Key Steps Involved in Operating Model Design

1. Scope	2. Drivers & Lenses	3. Apply	4. Design	5. Transform
Agree the Scope and Purpose of the Operating Model	Understand the Drivers and Choose the Most Relevant Lenses	Apply the Lenses to Organizational Elements	Design the Future State Model	Identify Areas Requiring Transformation

Step 1: Agree the model's scope & purpose

Good Operating Model Design Starts with a Clear Scope and Purpose

- When designing any operating model, it is important to agree the scope and purpose of the model:
  - What is the objective of producing the operating model?
  - To fulfil this aim, what is the scope that needs to be incorporated?
- Whilst operating models are used extensively for organization design and structuring, they can often be used to solve smaller, more contained challenges:
  - How should the organization be aligned to execute a complex end-to-end process that involves functions, geographies, people, process, technology and data?
  - How should a cross-organizational center of excellence or capability be established and incorporated into the broader organization to be most effective?
- In addition, agree upon the level of detail required, and the form of end deliverable desired. An operating can be a single piece of paper, or many hundreds depending on the level of detail necessary. A clear scope also ensures that data collection and analysis is targeted and sufficient.

Expert Tip!
Be conscious of the time and resources available to develop the operating model – this will heavily influence the level of detail that can be produced.

Expert Tip!
Developing an initial high-level operating model can be a useful starting point when the objective is not clear across stakeholders. This can then be used to iterate and drill deeper into areas of interest or concern.

Step 2: Understand drivers & choose lenses

Drivers and Lenses Inform Analysis and Model Design

- Understand the "problem being addressed", the purpose of the model and the drivers and factors most important to the operating model exercise. Internal and external factors should be explored across organization, process, people, controls, markets, technology, geographies. Examples of drivers and factors include:

  - Cost pressures, market growth, organizational inefficiencies, competition, geographic expansion.

- Once the high level drivers are identified, consider the best lenses to be used in the analysis and model development. The most appropriate lens to choose will depend on the problem being addressed, the aim of the operating model and stakeholders requirements (what do they want to see?). Examples of lenses include:

  - Customers, segments, channels;

  - Services, processes, capabilities;

  - Functions, teams, geographies;

  - People, roles, structure;

  - Systems, technology, infrastructure.

It's typical that an operating model will be developed with consideration of multiple lenses.

Step 2: Understand drivers & choose lenses

Consider the Key Drivers in Operating Model Analysis and Design

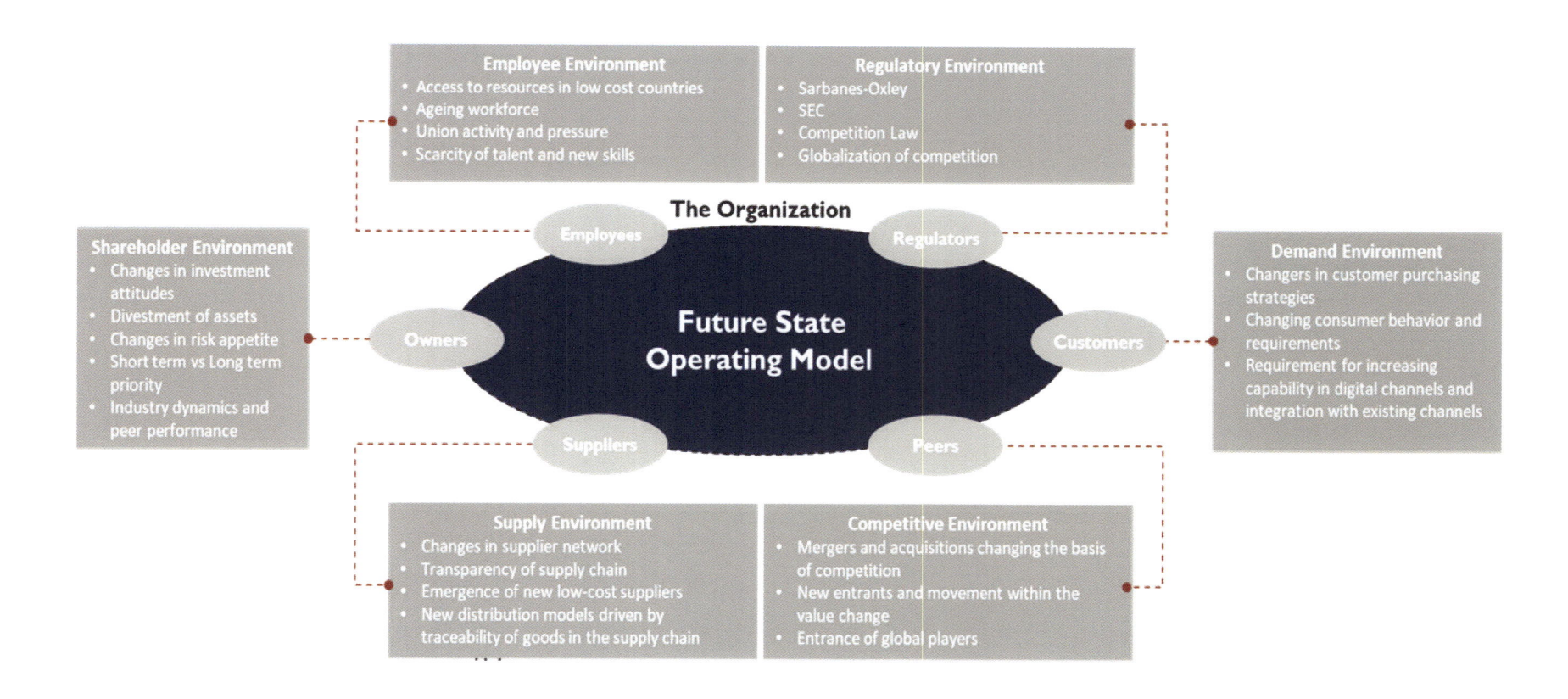

Employee Environment
- Access to resources in low cost countries
- Ageing workforce
- Union activity and pressure
- Scarcity of talent and new skills

Regulatory Environment
- Sarbanes-Oxley
- SEC
- Competition Law
- Globalization of competition

Shareholder Environment
- Changes in investment attitudes
- Divestment of assets
- Changes in risk appetite
- Short term vs Long term priority
- Industry dynamics and peer performance

Demand Environment
- Changers in customer purchasing strategies
- Changing consumer behavior and requirements
- Requirement for increasing capability in digital channels and integration with existing channels

Supply Environment
- Changes in supplier network
- Transparency of supply chain
- Emergence of new low-cost suppliers
- New distribution models driven by traceability of goods in the supply chain

Competitive Environment
- Mergers and acquisitions changing the basis of competition
- New entrants and movement within the value change
- Entrance of global players

The Organization surrounds the **Future State Operating Model**, connected via: Employees, Regulators, Owners, Customers, Suppliers, Peers.

Developing an operating model can be an iterative process – with aspects evolving over time. Priority should be placed on the most critical elements.

Step 3: Apply the lenses

Gather Information and Conduct Analysis Across the Lenses

- Conduct the necessary analysis which will inform the design of the model. Analysis will focus on the agreed lenses and will depend significantly on time / resources available and the existence of useable information.

- Approaches can incorporate data collection and analysis, current state model analysis, focused interviews, workshops, benchmarking, customer surveys and financial performance analysis.

- Gather data widely and talk to a variety of internal and external stakeholders to assist forming a balanced and comprehensive understanding across business challenges, drivers, objectives and plans for the agreed lenses.

- Depending on the extent of information currently available (including current state operating model), and the depth required in the model design, more extensive analysis may be require across organization, process, people, technology. This analysis could include such methods as SWOT Analysis, PEST Analysis, Porters Five Forces, Process Analysis and Capability Analysis (among many others).

Step 4: Design the model

Utilize the Analysis to Design the Model

- Build the model using the analysis conducted and applying principles of "good operating model design".
    - Place the end customer / front-office (store, channel, web, etc) at the opposite end to the back-office functions (warehouse, factory, etc)
    - Group dependent and related components close to another
    - Good operating models should not need extensive explanation
    - Allow the Operating Model to evolve and iterate as it is developed through discussions with stakeholders
    - Similarities across elements should be "connected" or "associated", differences should be "separated"
    - Utilize terms that resonate with the entire organization – minimize the introduction of new language
    - Consider using the value chain or "mega processes" of the organization to help with the layout of the Operating Model
    - Utilize different colors to help convey different messages and highlight critical areas of importance

Remember – there is no single right version of any operating model

Step 4: Design the model

Items to Consider when Developing a Future State Operating Model

- Use focus interviews and workshops to align key stakeholders on an agreed set of design principles for the new model

- Use case studies to look at peer organizations (or functions) in the sector or organizations in other sectors that are admired for their excellence

- Explore model design options using a variety of visualization techniques in order to describe what the new organization / entity / function would look like

- Test operating model options against the design principles and seek feedback from stakeholder in 1:1 discussions and workshop settings

- Utilize ranking mechanisms to evaluate model options against agreed design principles and overall business value / complexity to execute

- Iterate the model through option evaluation until a final preferred model is agreed

A good model enables stakeholders to explore options & decide on the way forward to maximize resource use, return on capital, business value & reduce risk.

Step 5: Identify transformation areas

Turning the Design into a Plan for Action

- In order for the operating model to take effect it will generally require a level of transformation or implementation.

- Using the lenses applied for the analysis and framing of the future state, design a transformation program:

  - How will the organization and inter-relationships need to change?

  - What skills, experience and expertise will be necessary in the future and how will these be changed?

  - How will processes, operations and systems need to be transformed to support the future state model?

  - What incentives need to be put in place to lead the organization to the new model and its effective operation?

  - What changes need to be made to business objectives and risk management models to make the model successful?

> **Whilst the operating model defines the future state, various transformation paths / options will exist for moving from the current state to the future state**

Examples of Operating Models

An operating model built on a value chain

Value chain: Develop Product Strategy & Offers → Market & Sell Products → Deliver & Manage Services → Manage Contracts → Manage Customers

		Business Strategy & Planning	Product Development & Sales	Service Strategy & Propositions	Marketing	Sales	Service Delivery	Contract Management	Customer Management
Central Head Office	**Strategic Direction**	Business Planning & Management; Forecasting	R&D; Product Strategy; PLM	Service Strategy; Alliance Strategy; Service Design	Marketing & Brand Strategy; Brand Management	Sales Strategy	Supply Chain Strategy; Procurement Strategy	Contract Portfolio Planning	Client Management Strategy
Regions & Divisions	**Business Management**	Business Leadership; Budgeting & Reporting	Portfolio Planning; Customization	Offer Development; Performance Analysis; Solution Design	Market Research	Sales Planning & Operations; Demand Generation	Supply Chain Planning; Scheduling	Contract Planning; Contract Risk Management	Client Management
Product Solutions Country Units	**Operations**	Business Management & Review; Business Support; Change & Comms	Pre & Post Sales Support; Product Support	Solution Development; Change Management	Market Development; Campaign Management	Salesforce Management	Resource Planning & Allocation; Performance Management	Contract Performance Management	Service Delivery Feedback

Example of a future state operating model

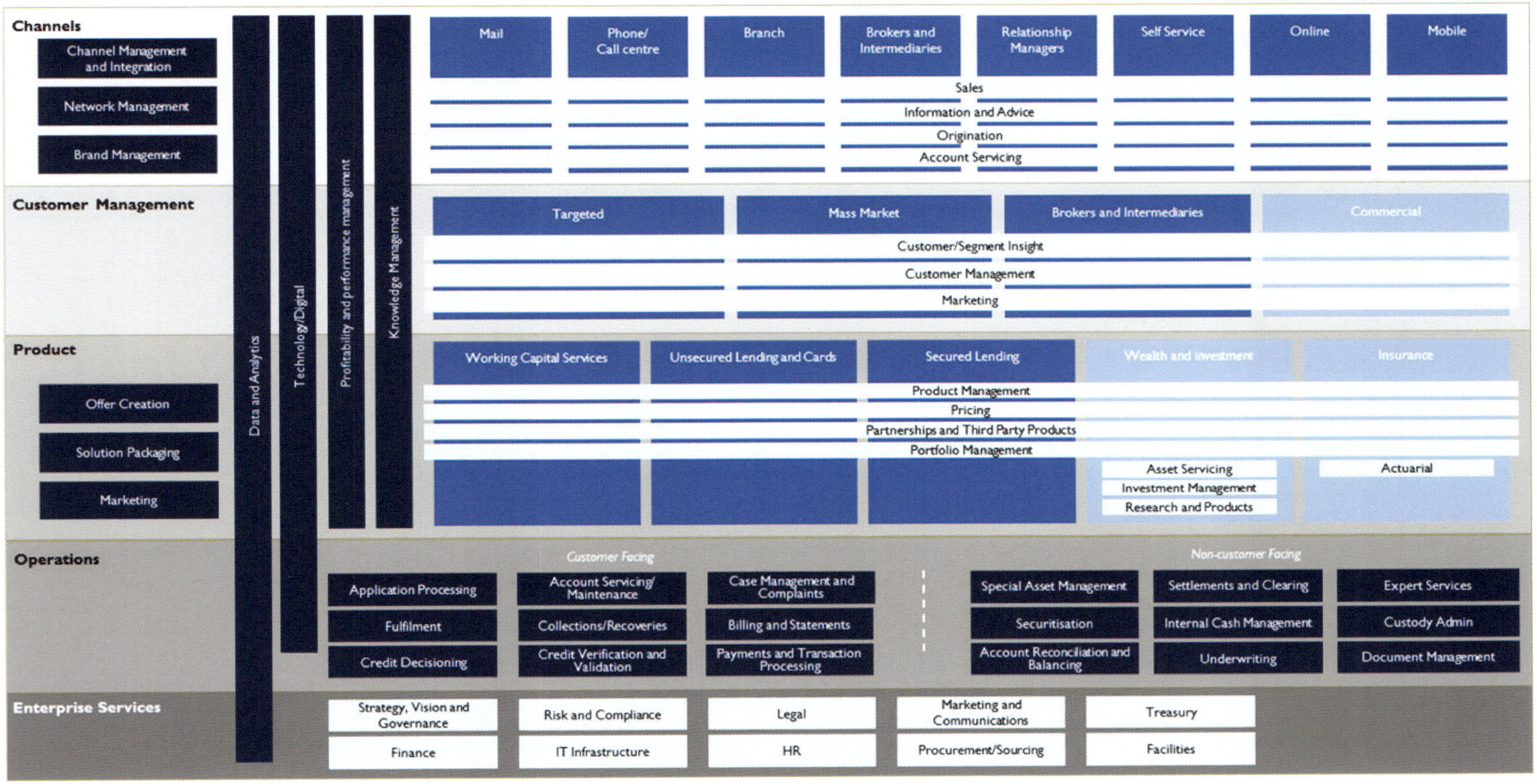

Channels
- Channel Management and Integration
- Network Management
- Brand Management

Mail	Phone/ Call centre	Branch	Brokers and Intermediaries	Relationship Managers	Self Service	Online	Mobile

Sales
Information and Advice
Origination
Account Servicing

Customer Management

Targeted	Mass Market	Brokers and Intermediaries	Commercial

Customer/Segment Insight
Customer Management
Marketing

Product
- Offer Creation
- Solution Packaging
- Marketing

Working Capital Services	Unsecured Lending and Cards	Secured Lending	Wealth and investment	Insurance

Product Management
Pricing
Partnerships and Third Party Products
Portfolio Management

- Asset Servicing
- Investment Management
- Research and Products
- Actuarial

Operations

Customer Facing

Application Processing	Account Servicing/ Maintenance	Case Management and Complaints
Fulfilment	Collections/Recoveries	Billing and Statements
Credit Decisioning	Credit Verification and Validation	Payments and Transaction Processing

Non-customer Facing

Special Asset Management	Settlements and Clearing	Expert Services
Securitisation	Internal Cash Management	Custody Admin
Account Reconciliation and Balancing	Underwriting	Document Management

Enterprise Services

Strategy, Vision and Governance	Risk and Compliance	Legal	Marketing and Communications	Treasury
Finance	IT Infrastructure	HR	Procurement/Sourcing	Facilities

Vertical columns: Data and Analytics | Technology/Digital | Profitability and performance management | Knowledge Management

Introduction to Financial Ratio Analysis

A valuable method for determining the performance of a company or the characteristics of a market

" *The competitor to be feared is one who never bothers about you at all, but goes on making his own business better all the time.* **"**

Henry Ford

Objectives of this Expert Toolkit Guide

1. Learn the fundamentals of financial ratio analysis and how it can add value in a business context

2. Learn the different types and categories of financial ratios and the specific ratios that exist in each category

3. Understand how to calculate a key set of critical financial ratios

4. Understand what insights might be revealed about a market or a company by calculating specific financial ratios

5. Learn the benefits and the limitations in financial ratio analysis and how ratios can be used to develop business hypotheses

An overview of financial ratio analysis

Financial Ratio Analysis can help determine the relative performance of a company:

- Ratio Analysis helps bridge the Income Statement, the Balance Sheet and Cash Flow

- Financial Ratio Analysis provides perspectives on three key corporate performance measures

- Current Profitability

- Return on Investment

- Financial Risk

- There are a range of financial ratio categories to consider:

Category	Aim
Profitability Ratios	Assess how efficiently companies are using their assets
Market Ratios	Utilize accounting and stock market data to derive value to shareholders
Long-term Debt and Solvency Ratios	Measure financial leverage of debt holders
Activity Ratios (Short and Long Term)	Help assess the efficiency of a company's operations
Liquidity Ratios	Determine a company's ability to repay creditors or lenders

Ratio analysis is a versatile tool for gaining strategic insight

Ratio analysis uses historical and comparable company data to assess performance:

- Ratio analysis can help identify areas of the company (operating, financing, or investing) which require corrective action in order to sustain or establish competitive advantage
  - Expose operational or organizational problems before they have a negative impact on performance
  - Disclose conditions which may develop into problems if not corrected
  - Financial ratio analysis can reveal potential problems many years before a company actually fails
- Ratio analysis can be used to select the optimum strategic direction when faced with a number of seemingly equivalent options
  - Ratio analysis can be used to simulate the outcomes of proposed plans and identify the most desirable strategy
  - This simulation can be used for both existing and start-up organizations

What can ratios tell us about a company?

When performing any sort of strategic or operational business analysis, ratio analysis can assist in the generation of potential hypotheses about a company or industry

Ratio	Calculation	What it Indicates
Gross Margin Percent (GM)	Net Sales - COGS] / Net Sales	• The extent to which a company exceeds direct product/service costs. • The extent to which a company is able to charge a price premium. • An indication of a company's procurement and production process efficiency.
Return on Sales (ROS)	Net Income / Net Sales	• The profitability of a company's operating activities.
Return on Total Assets (ROA)	Net Income / Average Total Assets	• How effectively a company's assets are being put to use. A very high ratio may indicate the company is close to maximum capacity.
Return on Investment (ROI)	Net Income Before Tax / Total Investments	• The relative performance of investments such as capital expenditures.
Return on Equity (ROE)	Net Income/Average Shareholder Equity	• Indicates what funds the company has for growth.
Return on Invested Capital (ROIC)	$(EBIT*(1\text{-tax rate}))/(\text{long-term liabilities} + \text{equity})$	• The return on the capital invested in the company, regardless of its source.

Financial performance and stock price

The relationship between financial performance and stock price

Ratio	Calculation	What it Indicates
P/E Ratio	Price Per Share / Earnings Per Share (EPS)	• Price investors are prepared to pay for each dollar of earnings
Market to Book Ratio	Price Per Share / Book Value Per Share	• Worth of company relative to how much shareholders have invested into it
Dividend Yield	Dividends Per Share / Price Per Share	• Return to an investor
Dividend Payout	Dividends / Net Income	• Portion of earnings paid out to shareholders
Market Capitalization	Stock Price x Common Shares Outstanding	• Equity value of company
Total Invested Capital (TIC)	Market Capitalization + Interest-bearing debt (including leases) + Preferred Stock	• Total value of company

Long-term debt and liquidity ratios

Long-Term Debt Ratios provide an understanding of the extent that debt capital been used to finance the assets of the company

Ratio	Calculation	What it Indicates
Debt to Total Capital	Total Debt / Total Capital	• Exposure to business risk and a measurement of financial leverage
Debt to Equity	Total Debt / Total Equity	• Measurement of financial leverage

Liquidity Ratios provide an understanding of whether a company can meet its short-term financial obligations when they are due

Ratio	Calculation	What it Indicates
Current Ratio	Current Assets / Current Liabilities	• Measure of a company's potential reservoir of cash
Quick Ratio	(Cash + Short-Term Securities + Receivables) / Current Liabilities	• Same as current ratio, but measures assets that are closer to cash
Times Interest Earned	EBIT / Interest	• The extent to which interest is covered by earnings – an indication of financial leverage

Activity ratios

Short-Term Activity Ratios indicate how efficiently a company manages its daily operations

Ratio	Calculation	What it Indicates
Working Capital Turnover	Sales / (Current Assets - Current Liabilities)	• Dollars generated for each dollar invested
Inventory Turnover	COGS / Average Inventories	• Could be a sign of efficiency or a sign of inventories being too low
Days Inventory On-Hand	365 / Inventory Turnover	• Number of days production (or sales) could continue with current inventory levels
Receivables Turnover	Net Sales / Average Accounts Receivable	• Used with inventory turnover to evaluate efficiency of working capital management
Days Receivables On-Hand	365 / Receivables Turnover	• How well a company is doing on collecting payments owed

Long-Term Activity Ratios indicate how efficiently a company utilizes its asset base

Ratio	Calculation	What it Indicates
Total Asset Turnover	Sales / Average Total Assets	Dollar sales generated per dollar invested in total assets
Fixed Asset Turnover	Sales / Average Fixed Assets	Dollar sales generated per dollar invested in property, plants and equipment

Ratios support hypothesis generation

When performing any sort of strategic or operational business analysis, ratio analysis can assist in the generation of potential hypotheses about a company or industry

Observation	Hypothesis
All companies in the industry have high margins	• The industry is of economic importance or provides a significant value added product
Some companies have low margins or are entirely unprofitable	• The industry is highly competitive or may be becoming obsolete
Company has high asset returns	• Manufacturing process may be labor intensive, workers may be highly skilled or assets may be aging
Inventory is significantly lower than industry norms	• The company may have more effective / efficient inventory management system
Inventory is significantly higher than industry norms	• The company may have inventory management challenges or may have an oversupply of (obsolete) products not in demand

These are indications only. See our guide on Hypotheses-based analysis to see how you might use these observations to develop and test hypotheses.

Ratios can help understand profitability

Financial ratios can help to gather insights into an organization's profitability

Question	Potential Insights
Is the company/industry adding significant value?	• High gross margin for all or most players
Is the industry highly competitive?	• Low gross margins • Some players unprofitable
Is the market / business price-driven?	• High Gross Margins • Profitability not closely correlated with volume
Is the market / business volume-driven?	• Low Margins • Profitability closely correlated with relative volume
Is this business operationally excellent?	• Higher profitability despite competitive pricing
Is the company differentiated through superior products, services, or customer relationships?	• Higher profitability driven by premium pricing

These are indications only. See our guide on Hypotheses-based analysis to see how you might use these observations to develop and test hypotheses.

Ratios can help understand productivity

Financial ratios can help to gather insights into an organization's productivity

Financial Ratio Observation	Potential Insights
High Inventory Turns / Cycles	• Fast, responsive business system • Product line focused on high turnover items • Could indicate that service levels are being compromised
High Asset Turns / Cycles	• Operating skill • Higher utilization • Lower marginal cost • Not investing in new technology • Aging assets
High Sales Per Employee / FTE	• Company leverages human resources effectively (sustainable) through business processes and technology • Company is cutting headcount to boost near-term results (not sustainable)

These are indications only. See our guide on Hypotheses-based analysis to see how you might use these observations to develop and test hypotheses.

Expert tips

Consider these Expert Tips when conducting Financial Ratio Analysis

- A company should always be evaluated on income from continuing operations. In other words, any special items should be removed before calculating the ratio. Special items may include restructuring charges, gains from the sale of assets and any other "one off" item.

- Always ensure that the ratio you are using makes sense for the company or industry you are analyzing. For example, inventory ratios are not likely relevant for a labor intensive services company.

- Always validate your calculation approach and confirm it with stakeholders involved in the analysis and the calculation approach most commonly used in that industry / region.

- Ratios are most powerful when compared over a time period (months, quarters, years) and when compared against industry peers (competitors).

Limitations

There are several limitations to consider when using financial ratio analysis

- Ratios can be significantly affected by:
  - Changes in accounting methods
  - Changes in accounting assumptions
  - Consolidation of a subsidiary's financial reporting into the parent company's financial statements
  - Acquisitions and divestitures during time period under analysis

- Ratio analysis does not indicate causality or give information as the cost drivers – so be cautious and use alternate complementary methods and data to verify any conclusions or hypotheses

- Financial ratio analysis is best considered a useful starting point for understanding a company's current situation

Note that some ratios are broader and some more specific and targeted

Some ratios are broader

- Profitability Ratios/Operating Performance:
    - Gross Margin Ratio = [Sales - COGS] / Sales
    - Return on Sales = Net Income / Sales
    - Return on Total Assets = [NI + After Tax Interest Exp.] / Avg. Total Assets
    - Return on Investment = Profit Before Tax / Total Investment
    - Return on Equity = NI / Average Equity Capital
    - Return on Net Assets = EBIAT / [Total Assets - Current Liabilities]
- Market Ratios:
    - P/E ratio = Price Per Share / Earnings Per Share (EPS)
    - Market to Book Ratio = Price Per Share / Book Value Per Share
    - Dividend Yield = Dividend per share / Price per share
    - Dividend Payout = Dividends / Net Income
    - Economic Value Added = [NI + Int. Exp.(1-TC)] / [Equity + Int. Bearing Debt]
- Long-Term Debt and Solvency Ratios:
    - Debt to Total Capital = Total Debt / Total Capital
    - Debt to Equity = Total Debt / Total Equity

Some ratios are specific / targeted

- Short-Term Activity Ratios:
    - Working Capital Turnover = Sales / (Current Assets - Current Liabilities)
    - Inventory Turnover = COGS / Average Inventory
    - Days Inventory on Hand = 365 / Inventory Turnover
    - Receivables Turnover = Sales / Average Accounts Receivable
    - Days Receivables on Hand = 365 / Receivables Turnover
    - Payables Turnover = Inventory Purchases / Average AP
    - Days Payables Outstanding = 365 / Payables Turnover
- Long-Term Activity Ratios:
    - Total Asset Turnover = Sales / Average Total Assets
    - Fixed Asset Turnover = Sales / Average Fixed Assets
- Liquidity Ratios:
    - Current ratio = Current assets / Current Liabilities
    - Quick ratio = [Cash+Mrkt. Sec.+AR] / Current Liability
    - Times interest earned = EBIT / Interest
    - Times int. earned (cash) = [EBIT + Depreciation] / Interest

Mastering Market Sizing & Share Analysis

Apply a proven analytical approach for determining the size of a given market and a company's share

> "I cannot give you the formula for success, but I can give you the formula for failure: Try to please everybody."
>
> — Herbert Bayard Swope

Objectives of this Expert Toolkit Guide

1. Explain the concepts of market share and market size and how they are relevant in a business context

2. Walk through the detailed approach and calculation methods for determining market size and market share

3. Outline the benefits and limitations inherent in market share and market size analysis

4. Provide Expert Tips to help you conduct market sizing and share analysis in an effective manner

Market Sizing Analysis

Introduction to market sizing analysis

The Purpose of Market Size Analysis

- Market sizing analysis allows us to quantify the size of a given market or segment by:
  - Value – revenue or profitability in a set period
  - Volume – units produced in a set period
- Done correctly, market sizing analysis brings value in various ways:
  - Determining the absolute and relative share of competitors in a business or segment
  - Insight into which competitors are doing well and not well in a market
  - The attractiveness of a business or segment including size, growth rates and relative attractiveness compared with other businesses or segments
- When doing market sizing analysis it's important to consider:
  - How the market sizing changes over time:
    - Historical: over a number of years
    - Forecast: projecting out over future years
  - Market size data may be available from third party sources, if not it must be estimated

© 2019 Expert Toolkit I ALL RIGHTS RESERVED I USAGE PERMITTED AS PER USER AGREEMENT   The Strategic Advisor Expert Bundle   Page 44

Market sizing analysis is a critical starting point for developing a business strategy

- Market sizing is used to determine the total current and future potential revenue for companies in a market across products and services within specified geographies and segments
- Market sizing aids strategic analysis:
  - Helps with sales forecasting and business case development
  - Provides insight into the phase of the industry life cycle and overall competitiveness of market
  - Provides insight into market attractiveness for entry exit consideration
  - Reveals the competitive landscape and a company's relative position
  - Supports the development of strategic hypotheses
- Knowing the size of the *addressable* market is essential:
  - Knowing which market components are unavailable will improve strategy development
  - For example, captive and regulated markets will have significant barriers to entry – and may not be available at all.

Market Sizing Strengths
- Provides a quantitative measure of business or segment attractiveness.
- Provides a key reference point against which market share and relative performance of competitors is measured.

Market Sizing Limitations
- Market sizing takes a significant investment in time, effort and resources.

Market sizing follows a three step process

Key Steps in Conducting a Market Sizing Analysis

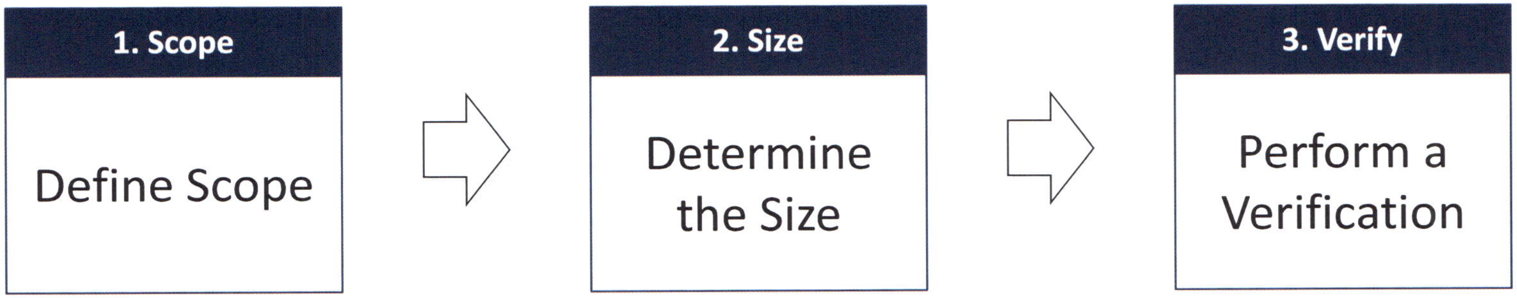

1. Scope	2. Size	3. Verify
Define Scope	Determine the Size	Perform a Verification

To do market sizing effectively it's important to complete all three steps in the process

Step 1: Define the scope of sizing analysis

Define the Industry and Market Scope

Before commencing the analysis, clearly define the scope and objectives:

- Identify the market for the products and services

- Utilize existing market segments when defining the scope (e.g. customer segments)

- Identify customer needs that are addressed by the products and services

    - Create a list of product attributes

    - Create a list of reasons why customer buy the products and services

- This will help to broaden the perspective beyond the typical industry definition which reveal potential "non-traditional" markets

- *Note: When non-traditional markets are identified, consider determining their size by looking at potential substitute or complementary products*

Expert Tip!
Ensure that all stakeholders agree with the scope and objectives of the analysis before proceeding!

A clear scope and set of objectives is critical when conducting a market sizing analysis as is ensuring the right resources and time has been allotted

Step 2: Determine market size

Two Broad Methods for Estimating Market Size

Sizing Based on Publicly Available Information

1. Utilize secondary references, such as analyst reports, to develop an initial estimate of the market size
2. Before using 3rd party sources, understand their methodology for sizing the market
3. Always interrogate their source data and confirm that it is reliable, sensible.
4. Obtain 2–3 independent estimates from different 3rd party sources and cross-check against each other.
5. Where differences exist, ensure that root causes are understood as are any underlying trends in market size.
6. Estimate the total market size
7. Validate total size and trends with industry experts.

Self Derived Market Size Estimate

1. Identify the key drivers of market size for the market in question, such as number of customers, number of units sold, average number of units purchased per customer, spend per customer.
2. Estimate the market size by using publicly available quantities such as customer populations, average spend and order volumes
3. Size the market based on a bottom-up approach or top down approach
   - Bottom-up looks at micro-variables such as number of customers
   - Top-down looks at macro-variables such as the aggregate size of related businesses

Step 3: Finalize size, determine addressability

Key Points for Sizing

- Consider all relevant data when developing the estimate
  - Sales volumes linked to imports and exports
  - Accessories, spare parts, repairs, replacements, service, maintenance, licenses
  - Upgrades, add-ons, contracts
  - Review competitor sales and growth rates to ensure market size and growth estimates are realistic
  - Identify key drivers of future market size such as macroeconomic trends, changes influencing customer demand and changes in number of customers, or average purchases per customer.

- Estimate the addressable market
  - Addressable Market = total market minus any captive and regulated portions
  - Served Market = addressable market minus unserved market
  - Market Share = total sales divided by addressable market

Expert Tip!
Ensure all extraneous and "one off" factors are removed from market size estimates and explicitly state the whether market size estimates are current or constant currency

Expert Tip!
Leverage all available data sources for information, such as internal company data (business plans, internal reports), annual reports, analyst reports, industry reports.

Step 3: Verify estimates

Verify, Verify, Verify

- Calculate the implied growth rate for the resulting market size estimate

  - Use compound annual growth rate (CAGR)

  - Compare implied growth rate versus historical growth rate over the same time period

  - Be sure to use deflated numbers when calculating growth rates if units are not available

  - Identify external factors that may have impacted the historical market growth rate and adjust market size and growth expectations accordingly

- It often makes sense to develop a top-down size estimate and a bottom-up estimate and compare each.

- Ensure the market size estimate is realistic for the size of the market in question

- Verify assumptions and market size estimates through multiple sources

  - Validate the market demand and supply are reasonable

  - Interview industry specialists to test assumptions and estimates

  - Test with any available market size assumptions and results

Expert Tip!
Cross-check all data (both publicly available market size data and own estimates).

Expert Tip!
Review market size estimate and assumptions with industry experts to justify (e.g., trade associations, investment banks, company personnel)

Final Expert Tips on Market Size and Growth Analysis

- Be sure to leverage existing and historical market size estimates as reference points.
- Compare market growth rates to other relevant growth rates: GDP, population, inflation, income, etc
- Consider factors that may impact growth rates such as inflation, market cycles, seasonality, stage of industry life cycle, long term trends, population changes, etc
- Identify external factors that may impact market demand in the future:
  - Customer segment growth rates
  - Changes in the number and location of customers
  - New competition or substitute products and services
  - Changes in the distribution models
  - Regulations and other political or macr-economic factors
  - Technological innovation
- Be sure to inquire into the causes of changes in total market size

Market Share Analysis

Why do we use market share analysis?

The Purpose of Market Share Analysis

- Market share analysis is an important method that can be used to:
  - Measure how much of a market or segment is held by specific competitors
  - Consider the absolute market share and relative market share when compared with other competitors
- Market share can be measured by:
  - Value: by total revenue or profit
  - Volume: by total units, orders, sales
- When done effectively, market share analysis can provide the practitioner with valuable insight:
  - The power of competitors relative to each other, customers and suppliers
  - How this power is changing over time
  - Which competitors are being successful
  - How new market entrants are performing
  - Any market imbalances that are being created by market share relativities

Getting market share analysis right

Determining Market Share

- There are several market share measures:

  - Absolute and relative share of the total market

  - Absolute and relative share of a segment

  - Absolute and relative share of total addressable market – in other words, segments in which the company competes

- Market share analysis helps to identify:

  - The degree of market concentration or fragmentation

  - The relative performance of competitors

  - The critical market issues that should be analysed further such as specific competitor performance drivers, advantages of holding a dominant share

Expert Tip!
Ensure consistent methodologies are used when measuring total market size and individual company or competitor share.

How to calculate market share

Various Market Share Measures

Measure of Share	How to Measure
Absolute Market Share – Total Market	Total Company Sales / Total Market Sales
Absolute Market Share — Specific Segment	Company Segment Sales / Total Segment Sales
Relative Market Share – Total Market	Total Company Sales / Total Sales of Largest Competitor
Relative Market Share — Specific Segment	Company Segment Sales / Largest Competitors' Segment Sales

Before Starting
- Determine the markets or segments to be sized
- Measure the performance of individual competitors in terms of sales, profits or units of output
- When measuring competitors utilize company analysis and financial analysis
- Ensure consistency between company measures and segment measure

The Fundamentals of Post- Merger Integration

Learn the core components, critical success factors and strategies for making a business integration successful

> "The successful warrior is the average man, with laser-like focus."
>
> — Bruce Lee

Objectives of this Expert Toolkit Guide

1. Provide an understanding of the drivers and implications of a merger in a business context

2. Share the fundamental approaches, timelines and stages involved in a merger and the related business integration

3. Describe the key questions to be asked during an integration and outline the key accountabilities and work-streams required to make an integration successful

4. Share lessons learned, best practices and tips for making a business merger successful

The purpose of mergers

Mergers are Initiated to Deliver Increased Shareholder Value

- There are 3 broad reasons, generally speaking, for a company to embark on a merger with another company:

Obtain Operational Synergies
(e.g. costs, productivity, quality, time, flexibility)

Drive Market Growth
(e.g. customers, new markets, market share, new countries)

Address Strategic Gaps
(e.g. products, technology, partners, markets, expertise)

Realizing synergies, achieving growth and closing strategic gaps are key to achieving the overall target of value creation

The value of disciplined merger integration

Mergers Managed Integrated, End-to-End Processes Deliver Greater Value

- Business mergers generally go through 6 stages from pre-deal through to post-deal

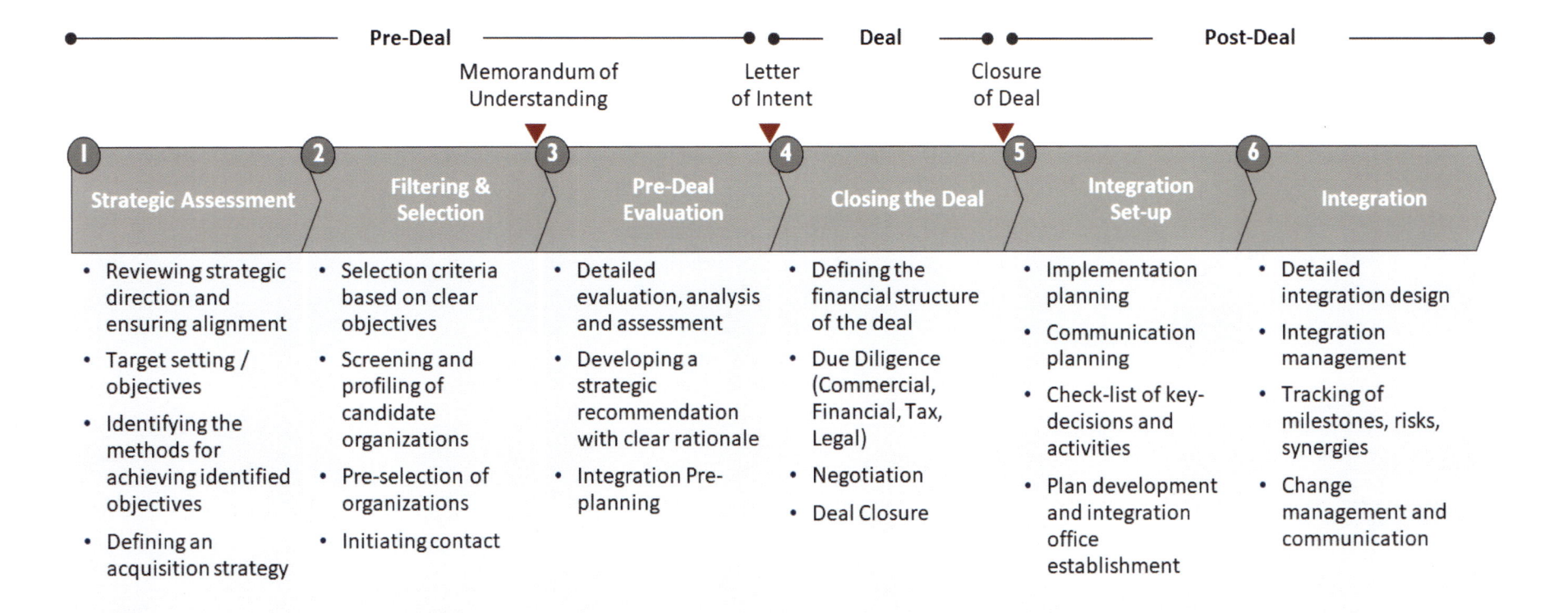

Pre-Deal — **Deal** — **Post-Deal**

Memorandum of Understanding | Letter of Intent | Closure of Deal

1 Strategic Assessment	2 Filtering & Selection	3 Pre-Deal Evaluation	4 Closing the Deal	5 Integration Set-up	6 Integration
• Reviewing strategic direction and ensuring alignment	• Selection criteria based on clear objectives	• Detailed evaluation, analysis and assessment	• Defining the financial structure of the deal	• Implementation planning	• Detailed integration design
• Target setting / objectives	• Screening and profiling of candidate organizations	• Developing a strategic recommendation with clear rationale	• Due Diligence (Commercial, Financial, Tax, Legal)	• Communication planning	• Integration management
• Identifying the methods for achieving identified objectives	• Pre-selection of organizations	• Integration Pre-planning	• Negotiation	• Check-list of key-decisions and activities	• Tracking of milestones, risks, synergies
• Defining an acquisition strategy	• Initiating contact		• Deal Closure	• Plan development and integration office establishment	• Change management and communication

The critical success factors of a merger

The Golden Aim: Securing Synergies and Minimizing Value Leakage

Common Causes of Integration Value Leakage

- Lack of executive alignment
- Organizational confusion and miscommunication
- Limited change management
- Lack of emphasis of cultural alignment and integration
- Insufficient planning and preparation
- Failure to realize critical synergies
- Ineffective integration performance measurement
- No explicit tracking of realized integration value
- Lack of resources and leadership attention on the integration (compared to the day-to-day)
- Lack of balance between operational and strategic integration

Elements Critical to Success

Detailed Planning	Program Management	Effective Decision Making
Cultural Integration	Change Management	Communication
Synergy Tracking	Allocated Resources	Talent Retention

Defining the degree of integration

Integration Options

A critical decision early in the process is the extent to which integration will occur between the organizations

Autonomy vertical axis (High to Low), Interdependence horizontal axis (Low to High):
- Preservation: High Autonomy, Low Interdependence
- Full integration: Low Autonomy, High Interdependence

- **Autonomy**
  - Is there a need to preserve distinct cultures after the merger?
  - Which capabilities, functions, key dimensions should be kept autonomous?
  - Can capabilities and functions be preserved in distinct sub-units or do they depend on broader organizational qualities?

- **Interdependence**
  - Is there a need for strategic interdependence among areas of the two companies?
  - Should interdependence be sought in specific capability or functional areas?

- **Choosing the Optimal Approach**
  - Which units / functions need strong autonomy?
  - Which units / functions require full integration?

A typical merger integration approach

Disciplined Integration Delivery is Critical to an Integration's Success

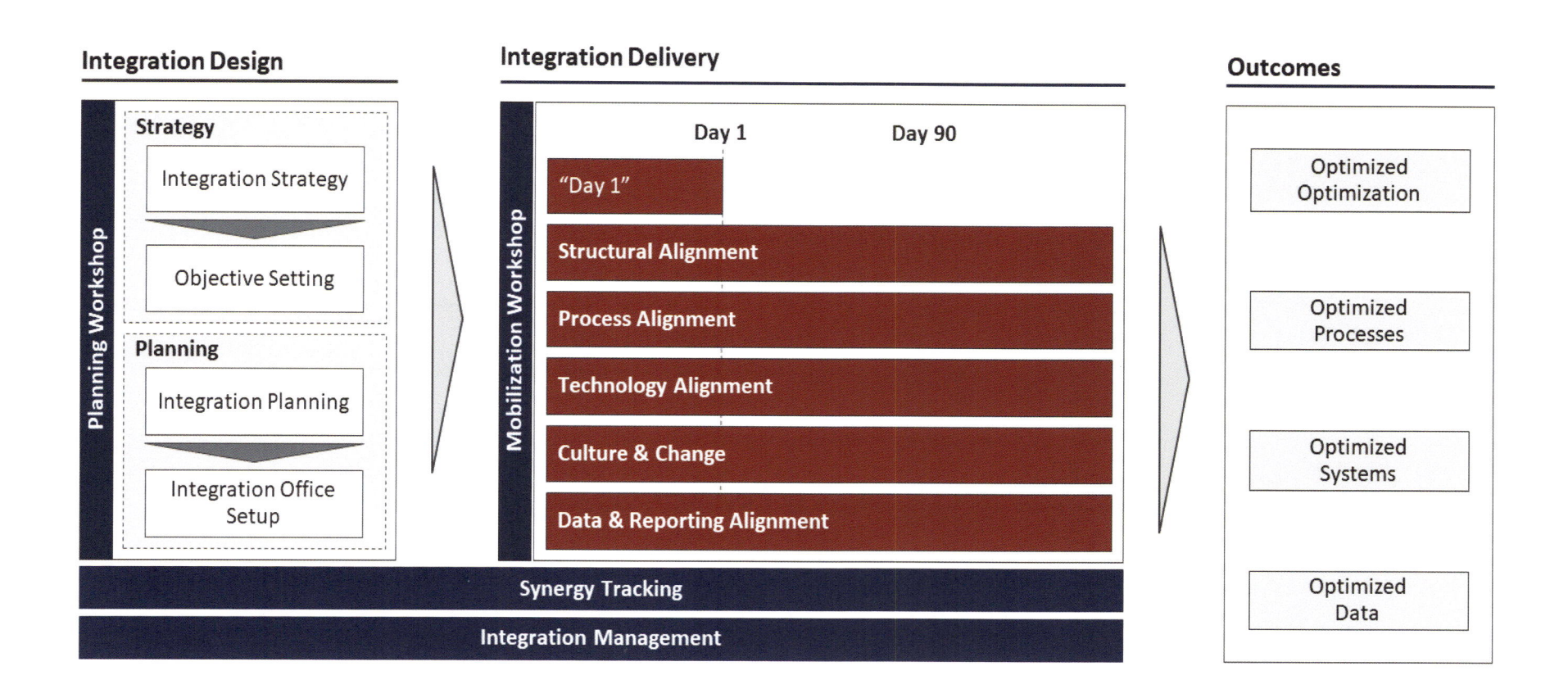

Integration Design

Planning Workshop

Strategy
- Integration Strategy
- Objective Setting

Planning
- Integration Planning
- Integration Office Setup

Integration Delivery

Mobilization Workshop

Day 1 → Day 90
- "Day 1"
- Structural Alignment
- Process Alignment
- Technology Alignment
- Culture & Change
- Data & Reporting Alignment

Synergy Tracking

Integration Management

Outcomes
- Optimized Optimization
- Optimized Processes
- Optimized Systems
- Optimized Data

Integration design – key components

Integration Design Must Identify the Key Elements Required

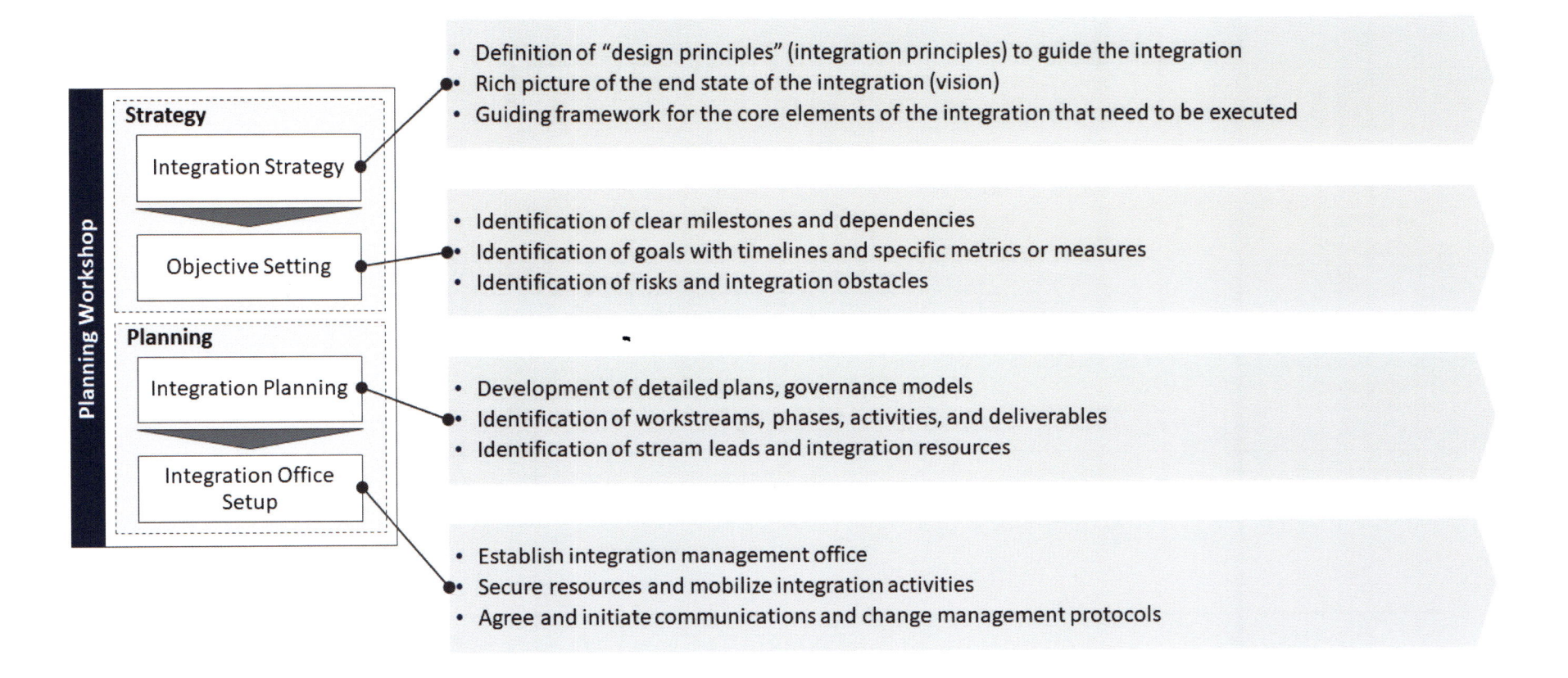

Planning Workshop

Strategy

- Integration Strategy

  - Definition of "design principles" (integration principles) to guide the integration
  - Rich picture of the end state of the integration (vision)
  - Guiding framework for the core elements of the integration that need to be executed

- Objective Setting

  - Identification of clear milestones and dependencies
  - Identification of goals with timelines and specific metrics or measures
  - Identification of risks and integration obstacles

Planning

- Integration Planning

  - Development of detailed plans, governance models
  - Identification of workstreams, phases, activities, and deliverables
  - Identification of stream leads and integration resources

- Integration Office Setup

  - Establish integration management office
  - Secure resources and mobilize integration activities
  - Agree and initiate communications and change management protocols

Integration design – key deliverables

Clear Objectives, Deliverables, Activities and Accountabilities is Essential

Strategic Milestone Plan

- A top level view of the key milestones that need to met during the integration.
- Clearly specifies activities, deliverables and timeframes involved.
- Identifies critical dependencies between activities and deliverables.
- Highlights key dates for major organizational changes, announcements and executive updates.

Detailed Integration Plan

- Detailed bottom-up project plans for the key streams of work that need to completed in key integration areas, such as systems, data, finance, processes, HR, operations, front-office.
- Needs to specify resource requirements, activities, milestones, dependencies and deliverables for each stream.

Integration Charters

- Concise charters outlining scope, success factors, objectives, measures, resources, operating rhythm, activities, governance, deliverables and dependencies for each integration stream.
- As a package, all stream integration charters together should encompass the entire integration effort and align with clear linkages.

Integration design – key questions

In designing a successful merger integration, it's important to address several key questions:

Legal
- What legal considerations do we need to incorporate into the merger process?

Business
- How will we position products, brand and services in the market?
- How will our customer and channel strategy need to be adjusted in the merged entity?

Operations
- How will we measure operational performance and the effectiveness of the operational integration?
- How do we maximize operational synergies and eliminate overlaps and redundancies?

Technology
- How will we integrate the systems and architecture across the merged organization?
- What are the critical time horizons that need to be accomplished for technology integration?
- What risks associated with data, security, access, business continuity do we need to manage?

Organization
- What will the future state operating model look like?
- How do we rapidly integrate key organizational areas? Which areas require more / less extensive integration?
- How we will ensure the retention of key personnel?

Integration management
- What will the integration management organization look like?
- What is the integration timeframe, milestones, dependencies and risks?
- How do we effectively manage the integration alongside day-to-day business operations?

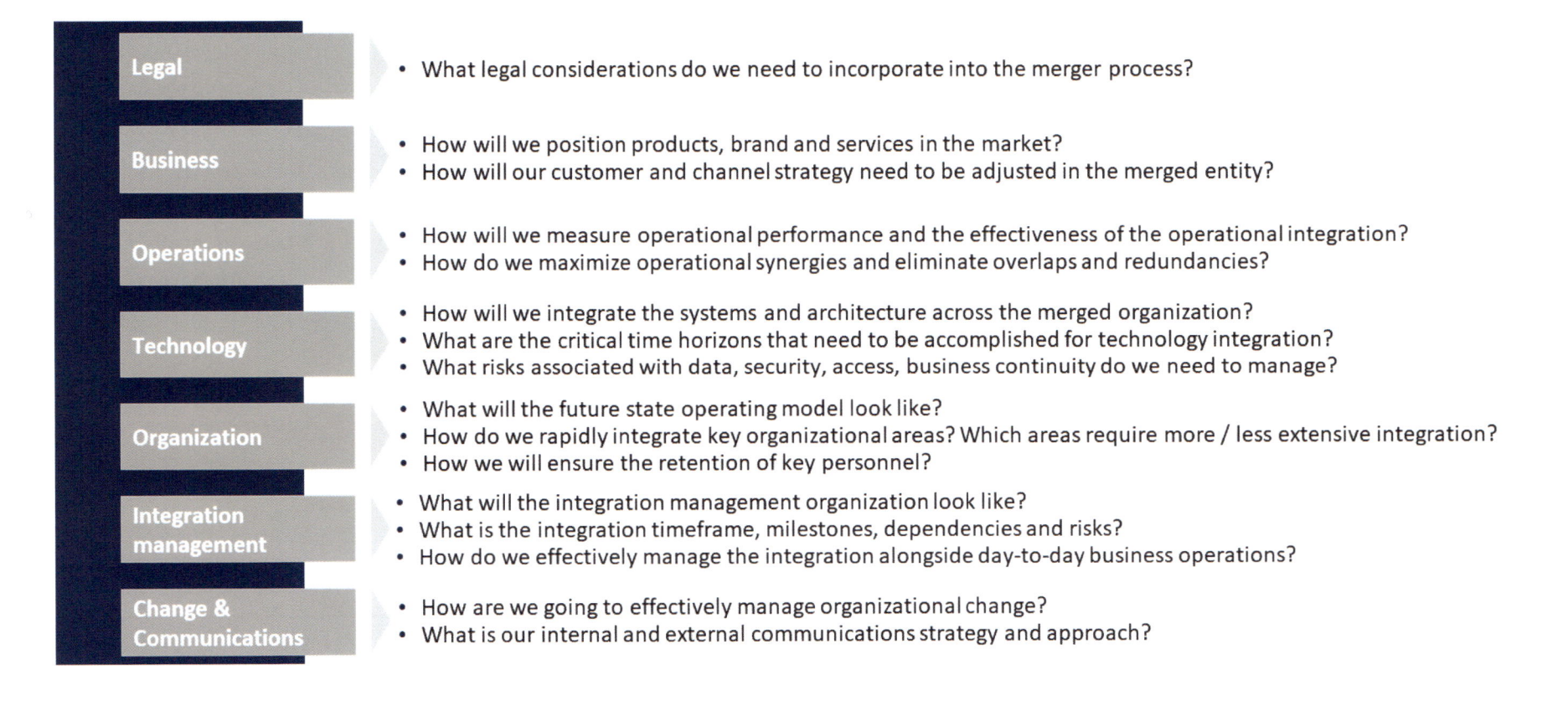

Change & Communications
- How are we going to effectively manage organizational change?
- What is our internal and external communications strategy and approach?

Integration delivery – key components

Integration Delivery Realizes the Objectives of the Plan

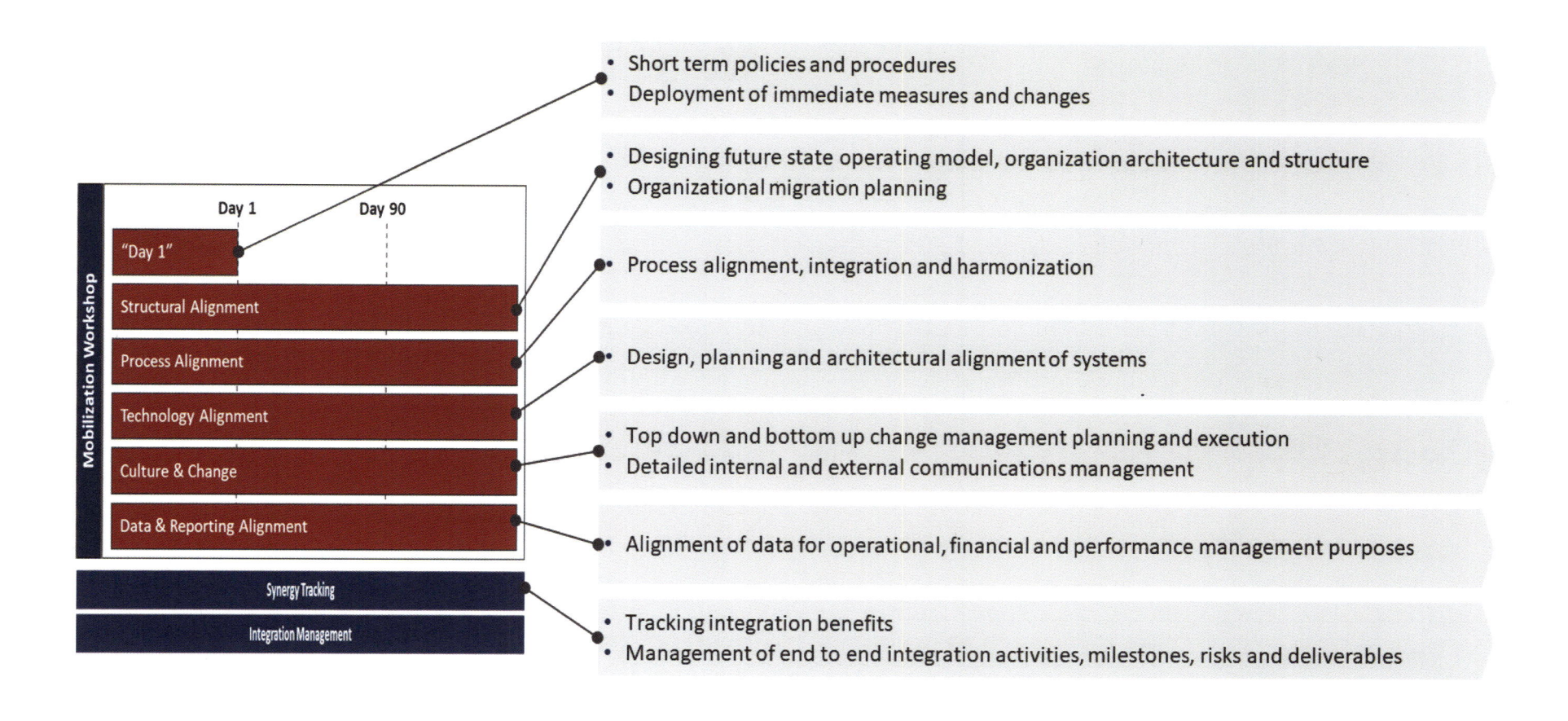

Mobilization Workshop timeline (Day 1 → Day 90):
- "Day 1"
- Structural Alignment
- Process Alignment
- Technology Alignment
- Culture & Change
- Data & Reporting Alignment
- Synergy Tracking
- Integration Management

"Day 1":
- Short term policies and procedures
- Deployment of immediate measures and changes

Structural Alignment:
- Designing future state operating model, organization architecture and structure
- Organizational migration planning

Process Alignment:
- Process alignment, integration and harmonization

Technology Alignment:
- Design, planning and architectural alignment of systems

Culture & Change:
- Top down and bottom up change management planning and execution
- Detailed internal and external communications management

Data & Reporting Alignment:
- Alignment of data for operational, financial and performance management purposes

Synergy Tracking / Integration Management:
- Tracking integration benefits
- Management of end to end integration activities, milestones, risks and deliverables

Integration delivery – structure and roles

Integration Requires a Robust Governance Structure

Complex business integration programs require clear governance, accountabilities, management processes and integration leadership to be successful.

Governance	Roles and Responsibilities
Steering Committee	• Guidance of integration strategy and objectives • Making critical decisions • Accountability for delivery of synergies • Escalations
Integration Management	• Day to day management of integration effort • Alignment of workstreams • Management of the plan and tracking benefits • Management of deliverables, activities, risks, issues
Workstream 1 **Workstream 1** **Workstream n**	• Delivery of workstream activities and deliverables • Raising issues and risks in a timely fashion • Allocation of management of workstream resources

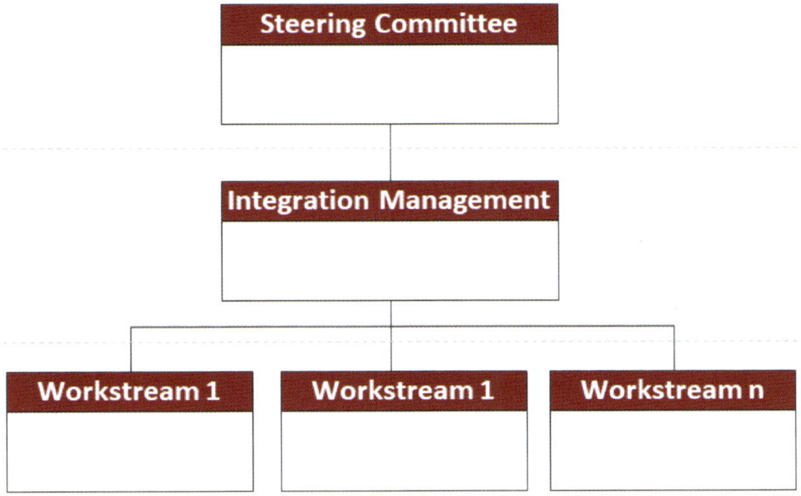

Expert Tips

Change Management & Communications

Expert Tip!
An integrated change management and communication plan outlining strategy, activities, responsibilities, timing, dependencies is critical.

Expert Tip!
A good communication plan should drive alignment across all key stakeholder groups including HR, operations, workplace relations / unions.

Expert Tip!
Utilize a range of communication methods throughout the course of the merger – including forums, newsletters, sessions, announcements, town halls, emails, online chat sessions, conference calls.

Expert Tips

Governance & Reporting

Expert Tip!
Utilize a consistent synergy forecasting, tracking and reporting process throughout the integration. Ensure the early involvement and endorsement of the Finance team in the process.

Expert Tip!
Integration plans should have sufficient detail on activities, deliverables and milestones for each workstream to allow appropriate transparency, tracking and control.

Expert Tip!
Regular and timely integration progress and performance tracking should include status of each workstream, results, risks and issues. Consistent reporting across workstreams should facilitate an integrated or rolled up view across the entire program.

Guide to Porter's Five Forces

A proven approach for assessing the market dynamics impacting an industry

"

The entrepreneur always searches for change, responds to it, and exploits it as an opportunity.

"

Peter Drucker

Objectives of this Expert Toolkit Guide

1. Provide an overview of the Porter's Five Forces Approach and outline how it adds value in a business context

2. Outline the four key steps involved in conducting a Porter's Five Forces Analysis

3. Provide detailed questions and considerations to use when conducting a Porter's Five Forces Analysis

4. Explain the benefits and limitations of Porter's Five Forces Analysis

An introduction to Porter's five forces

Porter's Five Forces is a framework for analyzing a company's environment or industry

- The Porter approach assumes that competition in any industry depends on five basic forces:

  1. Bargaining power of suppliers;

  2. Bargaining power of buyers;

  3. Threat of substitute products or services;

  4. Threat of new entrants to the industry; and

  5. Level of competitive rivalry between existing players

- The attractiveness of any industry is determined by the underlying causes of the structure and relative power distribution in that industry.

- The competitive position of a company within an industry is determined by the strengths and weaknesses of the company relative to the critical success factors for that particular industry.

- The development of competitive strategy relies on identifying a defensible competitive position in an industry that capitalizes on strengths and minimizes weaknesses of the organization.

Reasons for using Porter's 5 forces analysis

3 Reasons or Situations Amenable to Using Porter's Five Forces Analysis

1. Assess market attractiveness on the basis of competition within an industry

2. Highlight areas in which industry trends may present opportunities or threats

3. Analyze where a company stands in relation to the the underlying causes of competitive forces

Key considerations exist in each of the five force categories

Several important economic and technical characteristics of an industry are critical to the strengths of each competitive force

Threat of New Entrants

Barriers to entry:
- Economies of scale (including shared resources).
- Product differentiation (proprietary).
- Capital requirements.
- Switching costs.
- Access to distribution channels.
- Cost disadvantages independent of scale.
- Government policy.

Bargaining Power of Suppliers

A supplier group is powerful when:
- It is dominated by a few companies and is more concentrated than the industry it sells to.
- There are no substitute products.
- The industry is not an important customer.
- Its products are important to the industry.
- Products are differentiated or suppliers have built up switching costs.

Intensity of Rivalry

Intense rivalry results from:
- Numerous or equally balanced competitors.
- Slow industry growth.
- High fixed or storage costs.
- Lack of differentiation or switching costs.
- Capacity augmented in large increments.
- Diverse competitors.
- High strategic stakes and High exit barriers.

Bargaining Power of Buyers

A buyer group is powerful when:
- It purchases large volumes relative to seller sales.
- The products represent a significant fraction of the buyers' costs or purchases.
- The products are standard or undifferentiated.
- It faces few switching costs.
- It earns low profits.
- The bought product is unimportant.

Pressure from Substitute Products

Are there products that can perform the same function?
What is the buyers' propensity to substitute?
Focus on those that:
- Are improving their price performance trade-off compared with the other products.
- Require low switching costs.
- Are produced by industries earning high profits.

Additional considerations related to barriers & competition

Consider Returns and Differentiation Approaches

New Entrant Financial Return Considerations

	Exit Barriers	
	Low	**High**
Entry Barriers — Low	Low, stable returns	Low, risky returns
Entry Barriers — High	High, stable returns	High, risky returns

Competition Considerations

	Competitive Advantage	
	Low Cost	**Differentiation**
Competition Scope — Broad	Cost Leadership	Differentiation
Competition Scope — Narrow	Cost Focus	Differentiation Focus

Understanding and responding to the forces

Once the Forces are understood, the response is to take offensive or defensive actions to create a defensible position against the forces

Position the company so that its capabilities provide the best defense

Influence the balance of forces through strategic moves

Anticipate shifts in the factors underlying the forces and respond to them

The four steps of a Five Forces Analysis

Key Steps in Developing a Five Forces Model

1. Macro Trend Analysis
Define the industry and scope of analysis

2. Industry Trend Analysis
Conduct a broad industry analysis

3. Trend Quantification
Identify the strategic groups in the industry

3. Trend Quantification
Identify the company's competitive position within its strategic group

Steps 1 and 2 are primarily directed at identifying the attractiveness of the industry and Steps 3 and 4 are aimed at determining the relative position in that industry

Step 1: Define industry & scope of analysis

The Scope of the Analysis Must be Defined at the Outset

- Identify the customer needs fulfilled by the company's products and services

  - This can be completed by outlining a list of product attributes and reasons "why customers buy our product"

  - Creating this list will broaden the perspective beyond the immediately obvious industry definition and will help to identify potential substitute products

- Defining the industry is an essential step to ensure tangible results from the five forces analysis

- Source industry level data:

  - Interviews with executives, industry experts, customers to determine the players in the industry

  - Trade associations, business press, trade journals, and electronic databases

Step 2: Conduct a broad industry analysis

The Industry Players and Their Relative Power Should be Determined

- Industry structure and relative strength of each player should be determined
  - Identify the players (e.g. competitors, buyers, suppliers, substitutes, new entrants)
  - Determine the relative strength of each player
  - Identify macroenvironmental trends that might impact these relationships in the future
- The relative strengths of these players is referred to as their bargaining power
  - Bargaining power is generally referred to as either
    - Strong - threats to the industry attractiveness
    - Weak - Opportunities to be exploited

To determine the bargaining power of each player, seek to answer the questions that appear on the following panels – for each competitive force

Step 2a: Determine supplier power

How is Power Allocated Across the Supply Chain?

- What is the amount of differentiation among inputs to the industry?

- What are the relative switching costs for suppliers and companies in the industry?

- Are substitute inputs readily available to the industry?

- How important is sales volume to suppliers in the industry?

- What is the concentration of suppliers relative to the concentration of companies in the industry?

- What are the cost of inputs relative to total industry purchases?

- What impact does the quality & cost of industry inputs have on total cost or differentiation?

- What is the threat of suppliers integrating forward relative to the backward integration of firms in the industry?

Step 2b: Determine buyer power

How is Power Allocated Across Buyers?

- What is the concentration of buyers relative to the concentration of companies in the industry?

- What percentage of total industry volume is purchased by individual buyers?

- What are the relative switching costs for buyers and companies in the industry?

- What information do buyers have about the industry's costs and prices? Can buyers use this information to negotiate more aggressively?

- What is the threat of buyers integrating backward relative to the forward integration of companies in the industry?

- Are substitute inputs readily available to buyers?

- What impact does the quality and cost of industry outputs have on total cost or differentiation for the buyers?

- How important is the brand identity of inputs to buyers?

- How important is the differentiation of inputs to buyers?

Step 2c: Determine threat of substitutes and new entrants

Are New Market Players and Products Possible?

- What is the relative price-performance value of existing substitutes?

- What are the costs of switching among various substitutes?

- What is the buyer propensity to substitute?

- What new, unforeseen or undeveloped substitutes are likely to become available?

- What economies of scale in operations, distribution, sales are necessary to be competitive?

- Do companies have proprietary differences in products or production?

- Is brand identity an important component of competition?

- What are the necessary capital requirements?

- Are distribution channels easily accessible to new entrants?

- What absolute cost advantages do existing companies have in this industry?

- What government policies and regulations act as barriers or restrict moving into, from, and within the industry?

- Can existing companies be expected to retaliate aggressively to new entrants?

Step 2d: Determine the level of competitive rivalry

What's the Extent of Market Competition?

- Has the level of industry growth been sufficient to allow companies to grow without competitive reprisal?

- Are fixed or storage costs large in comparison to the value added to the product or service?

- What significant differences exist among the products and services offered by the companies in the industry?

- Is brand identity an important differentiation factor?

- Are there high switching costs?

- What is the concentration of companies and is there balance among them?

- How diverse are the competitors? Are operations subsidized in this industry with profits from another?

- What is at stake from a corporate perspective? The entire company, a business unit or just a pilot operation?

Step 2e: Review trends to understand industry dynamics

Assess Market Dynamics

The answers to these questions regarding the five competitive forces provides a 'static' picture of the structure and nature of competition in the industry.

- To understand the 'dynamics' of these forces, review the macroenvironmental trends that are likely to impact the current and future structure of the industry, using a PEST Analysis:

  - Political

  - Economic

  - Social

  - Technological

- Data for this trend analysis should come from both internal and external sources

  - The internal sources include executive and employee interviews, data from cost systems and detailed support data for financial budgets.

  - The external sources include interviews with industry experts, industry summary report and detailed data from trade associations

Step 3: Identify the strategic groups in the industry

Identify Strategic Groupings to Develop a More Focused Strategy

- A strategic group is a group of companies in an industry that follow the same or similar competitive strategies
  - An industry could have one strategic group if all the companies followed the same strategy
  - Alternatively, each company in an industry could be in its own strategic group
- In general, strategic groups with fewer competitors have a greater likelihood of earning higher profits.

Step 3a: Define strategic groups by looking for similarities

Identify Strategic Groupings to Develop a More Focused Strategy

Strategic groups are revealed through similarities along key strategic dimensions:

- **Specialization** – the degree of focus in product line, target customers and geographies served

- **Brand Identification** – the degree of product differentiation sought based on image

- **Push versus Pull** – the degree to which distribution channels play a role in selling the product

- **Channel Selection** – the choice of distribution channels

- **Product Quality** – the level of product quality in terms of materials and features

- **Technological Leadership** – the degree to leadership versus following and imitation

- **Vertical Integration** – the extent of value added attributable to vertical integration

- **Cost Position** – the extent to which a low cost manufacturing and distribution is sought

- **Service** – the degree to which additional services are provided with the product

- **Price Policy** – the relative price position in the market

- **Leverage** – the amount of financial and operating leverage it carries

- **Relationship with Parent** – the degree of resources and costs sharing with the parent

- **Relationship with home and host government** – the level of resources and support provided

Step 3b: Use a strategic map to identify groups

Strategic Map Development

- A strategic map is developed by identifying the *two* most critical dimensions driving performance in the industry
  - These critical dimensions can be determined through interviews with internal and external industry experts or through a detailed critical success factors analysis

- Each competitors' relative strength or weakness on the two dimensions is determined and plotted
  - Competitors' position on the two critical dimensions can be determined through interviews with industry experts or a detailed S.W.O.T. analysis

- After the strategic groups are formed, a validation check should be performed to ensure that companies in the same strategic group have similar strategies
  - Verify the impact of external events or competitor moves on the companies in the same strategic group
  - If all competitors in a group are affected in a similar way, the proposed strategic grouping is most likely logical

Step 4: Determine competitive position in the strategic group

Competitive Positioning

Once strategic groups have been identified, the relative strengths and weaknesses of each competitor should be identified.

- The strengths-weaknesses analysis could be conducted by rating the company relative to each competitor on the critical success factors in the industry

- The analysis should be performed by creating a matrix with the critical success factors on the vertical axis and the competitors in the strategic group on the horizontal axis

- The rating given should be one of the following:

    − **+** = company is better than competitor

    − **-** = company is worse than competitor

    −**o** = company is the same as the competitor

Additional considerations and reminders

Expert Insights

- Additional strategic opportunities may arise from the secondary review of the impact of the competitive forces on each strategic group.

- **Opportunities** are defined as:
  - The creation of a new strategic group
  - Shifting to a more favorably positioned strategic group
  - Strengthening the structural position of an existing group

- **Threats** are defined as:
  - Risk of other companies entering the strategic group
  - Factors that reduce the mobility barriers of a company's strategic group
  - Decreasing power with customers or suppliers
  - Risk of faulty investments necessary to improve a company's position

An Introduction to PEST Analysis

An essential analytical tool for understand market dynamics and informing a business strategy

> "The entrepreneur always searches for change, responds to it, and exploits it as an opportunity."
>
> — Peter Drucker

Objectives of this Expert Toolkit Guide

1. Provide an overview of the PEST Analysis approach and outline how it adds value in a business context

2. Explain how PEST Analysis and Porter's 5 Forces work together

3. Outline the key steps involved in producing a PEST Analysis

4. Introduce templates to use for conducting PEST Analysis

5. Explain the value of PEST Analysis and provide Expert Tips to maximize its value

6. Provide an example of PEST Analysis

An Introduction to PEST analysis

What is PEST Analysis?

PEST is an analytical approach that helps to determine the influence of macro-environmental trends in markets where a company operates and competes. There are four primary macro-environmental trend categories considered:

Trend Categories	Examples
Political trends determine the likely outcome from a government legislative or regulatory body	Industry regulation or deregulation, environmental or tax legislation, monetary policy (tight vs. loose), tariffs, domestic-content rules, license requirements, legal opinions.
Economic trends include broad measures of economic health	GDP growth, unemployment levels, inflation, foreign currency exchange rates, balance of trade, credit rates, availability of skilled labor and raw materials.
Social trends reflect cultural and demographic influences	Culture includes clothing fashions, buying habits, consumer behavior. Demographics includes age, income, education, and geographic location of customers and employees.
Technological trends include innovations that impact products, processes and market dynamics	Technologies in the design of physical product or information flow surrounding the physical product, design of production processes.

The PEST framework

What is the PEST Framework?

- The PEST framework outlines the characteristics of each of the 4 macro-environmental forces mentioned on the previous page:

  - Political

  - Economic

  - Social

  - Technological

- It explains how these forces affect:

  - the competitive landscape

  - a company's value chain

  - a company's financials

- The PEST Framework is typically used in conjunction with other industry analysis frameworks to help explain ongoing changes in the industry and determine how they might impact a business.

Using PEST analysis and Porter's 5 Forces

PEST analysis provides a lens on macro-environmental trends, Porter's 5 Forces helps understand industry trends

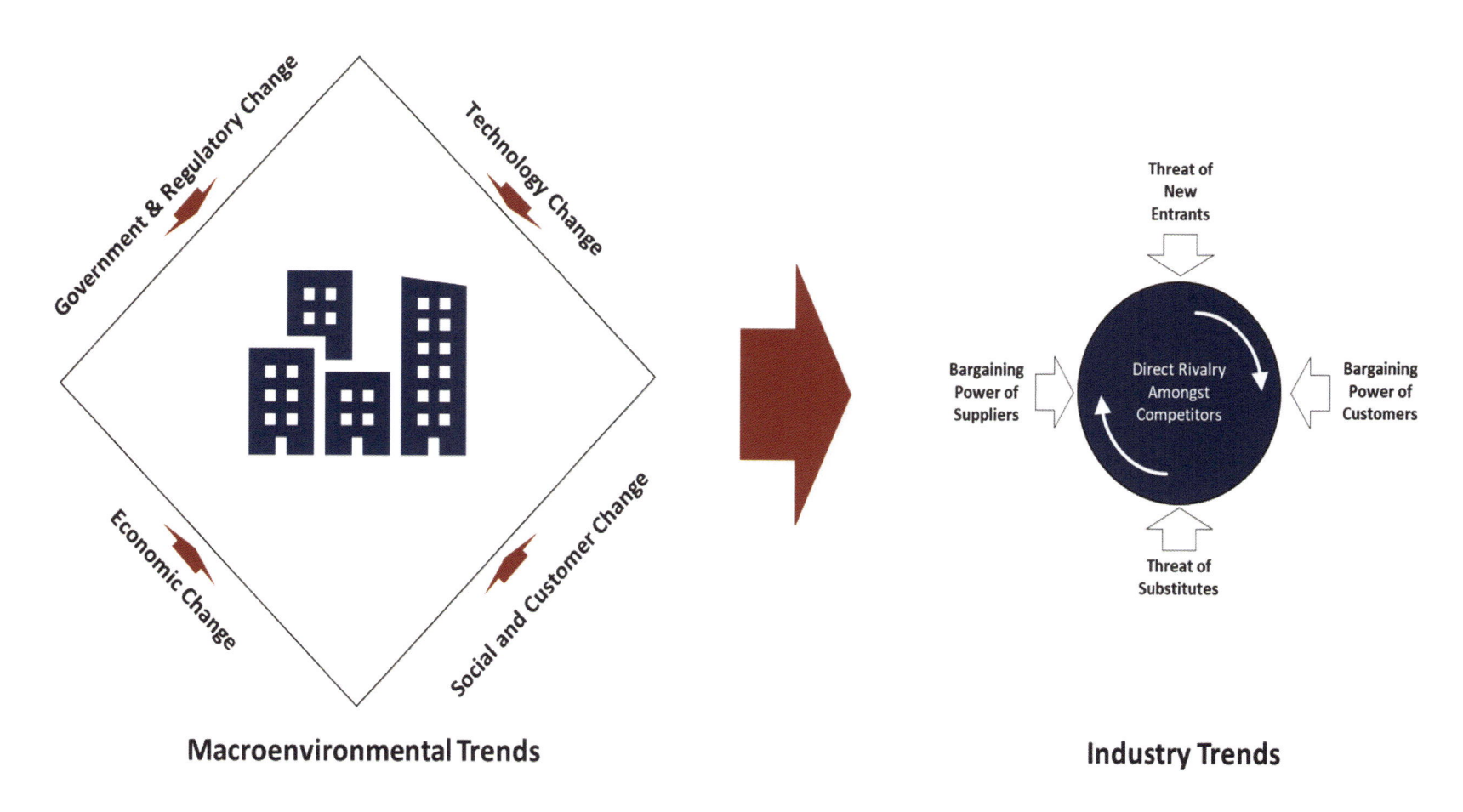

Macroenvironmental Trends
- Government & Regulatory Change
- Technology Change
- Economic Change
- Social and Customer Change

Industry Trends
- Threat of New Entrants
- Bargaining Power of Suppliers
- Direct Rivalry Amongst Competitors
- Bargaining Power of Customers
- Threat of Substitutes

Key steps in developing a PEST model

There are 4 steps in Developing a PEST Model

1. Macro Trend Analysis	2. Industry Trend Analysis	3. Trend Quantification	4. Present Results
Utilize primary research and secondary research – both quantitative and qualitative. Assess Opportunities and Threats	Understand and analyze the industry structure and competitive environment.	Evaluate the trends and attempt to numerically quantify them.	Summarize and present the results

Step 1: Macro Trend Analysis

Trend Analysis Begins with Data Collection

- Environmental trend analysis involves an extensive data collection effort
- To focus trend analysis, begin with an analysis of competitor trends and behaviors:
  - Limit the number of competitors analyzed to a relevant sample to ensure the necessary level of detail is reached
  - Identify the number, size, consolidation, vertical integration and rivalry of competitors in the markets under analysis
  - For each competitor, focus on the relevant characteristics, actions, strategies:
    - Capabilities
    - Offers / Products / Services
    - Capacity utilization
    - Cost structures
    - Operating Model
    - Strategy
    - Financials
    - Partnership Strategies
- Use this to identify associated macroenvironmental trends (Political, Economic, Social, Technological)

Step 1: Macro Trend Analysis

Identify economic influences in the market

The trends specific to markets under analysis should be identified, including:

- Size and growth rate of the market
- Cyclicality
- Seasonality
- Segmentation
- Product differentiation
- Price sensitivity

- Customer needs
- Availability of substitutes
- Potential entrants
- Barriers to entry and exit
- Supplier relationships
- Industry profitability

Step 2: Industry trend analysis

Assess the Impact on Industry and Competitive Dynamics

- Use Porter's "Five Forces" framework, identify the impact of macroenvironmental trends on the industry and competitive dynamics

- The influence of each trend should be assessed

- The likelihood the trend will continue in the future should also be determined

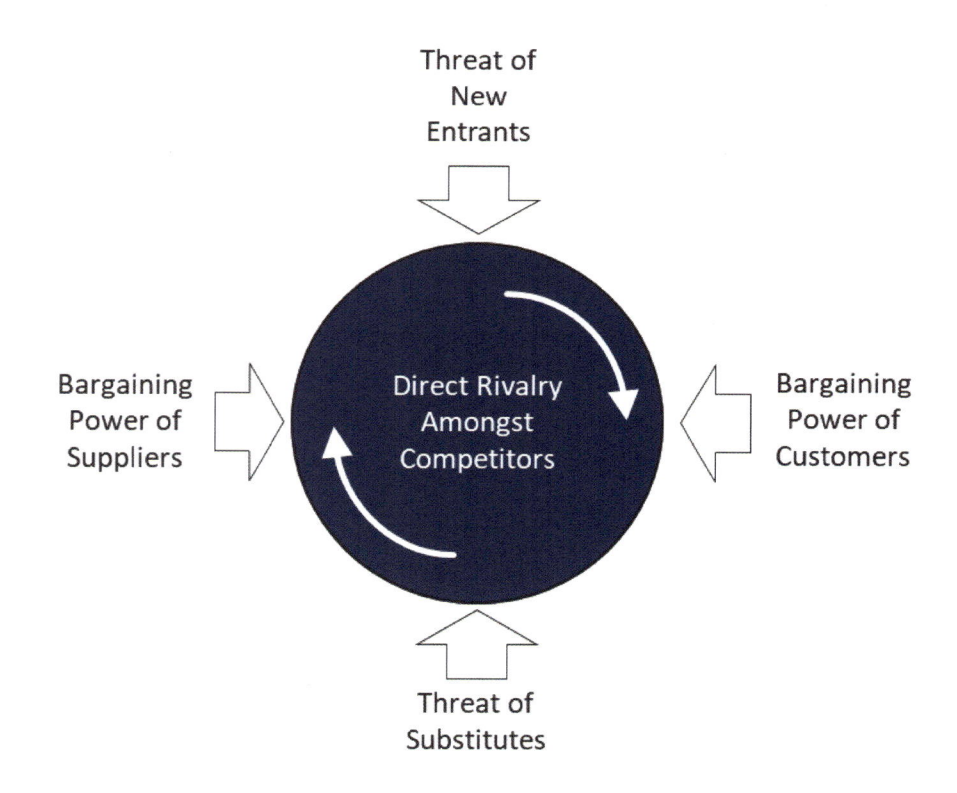

Threat of New Entrants

Bargaining Power of Suppliers

Direct Rivalry Amongst Competitors

Bargaining Power of Customers

Threat of Substitutes

Step 3: Trend quantification

Trends Should Be Quantified Where Possible

- If possible, the identified trends should be quantified
  - Plot the "raw" data over time to identify seasonal or cyclical trends
  - Use visual analysis and regression to observe relationships
  - Calculate the annual growth rate and plot over time
  - Verify the quantified results merit the trend being a relevant factor

$$\%Change_{t+1} = \frac{\left(Value_{t+1} - Value_t\right)}{Value_t}$$

Step 4: Present the results

A Trend Summary Matrix can be used to Present the Results of the Analysis

#	Key Market Trends	Evidence or Observation of Trends	Implications		Strategic Hypotheses	Competitive Advantage Gained?
			Opportunities	Threats		
1.						
2.						
3.						

The Complete Picture

Bringing it all Together

Step 1. Macroenvironmental Analysis (Opportunities)

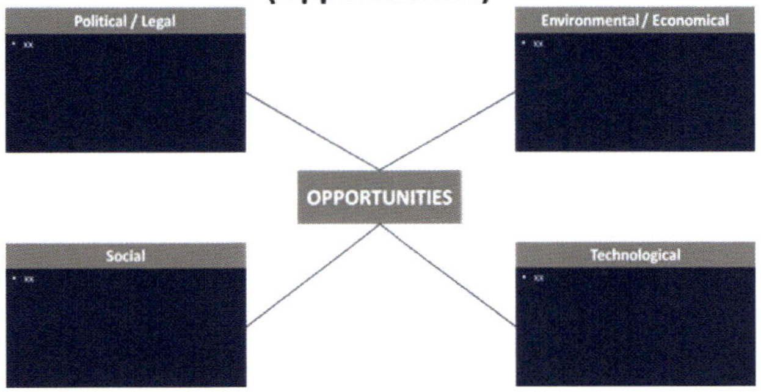

Political / Legal
- XX

Environmental / Economical
- XX

OPPORTUNITIES

Social
- XX

Technological
- XX

Step 1. Macroenvironmental Analysis (Threats)

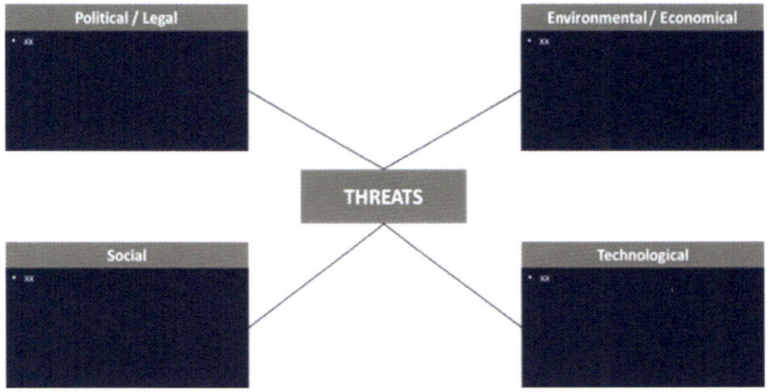

Political / Legal
- XX

Environmental / Economical
- XX

THREATS

Social
- XX

Technological
- XX

Step 2. Industry Analysis

Threat of New Entrants
- XX

Bargaining Power of Suppliers
- XX

Rivalry Among Existing Competitors
- XX

Bargaining Power of Customers
- XX

Threat of Substitutes
- XX

Step 4. Trend Summary Matrix

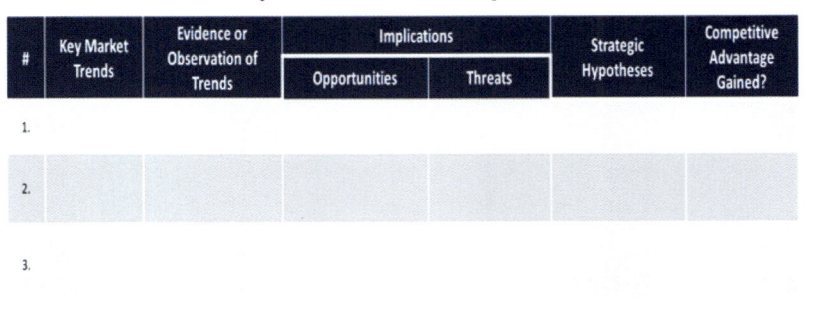

#	Key Market Trends	Evidence or Observation of Trends	Implications		Strategic Hypotheses	Competitive Advantage Gained?
			Opportunities	Threats		
1.						
2.						
3.						

The value of PEST analysis

PEST Analysis is a Valuable Technique in Many Business Situations

- It provides a good, structured framework for conducting an overall scan of the macro-environment in the initial stages of strategic planning and analysis exercises.

- It is a good method for identifying the value drivers, critical success factors and dynamics at play within a given industry.

- It is a sound preparation exercise providing input to more extensive strategic development initiatives such as scenario planning, game theory and strategy development.

- It is flexible and adaptable allowing a more extensive analysis to be performed or a more high level analysis to be performed in cases where time and resources may be restricted.

Expert Tips for using PEST Analysis

Tips

- PEST can lead to quite qualitative and subjective insights and results, so they should not be relied-upon exclusively for conducting analysis and developing business strategies.

  - Be sure to combine PEST analysis with other analytical methods to ensure findings and conclusions are sound.

- PEST analysis can require extensive time and resources in addition to a significant data collection effort.

  - Be sure to allow for the appropriate time and effort when using this method. It is recommended to develop a clear plan with an agreed scope, milestones, resources and accountabilities before commencing the PEST analysis exercise.

- It is important to engage with a range of stakeholders, garnering their input on scope, objectives, perspectives and insights.

  - Be sure to highlight any contradictory inputs and findings and agree with the key steering members on the appropriate course of action (compromise, exclusion, average, etc).

Example & Template
PEST Analysis + Porter's Five Forces

PEST Analysis Example – Threats

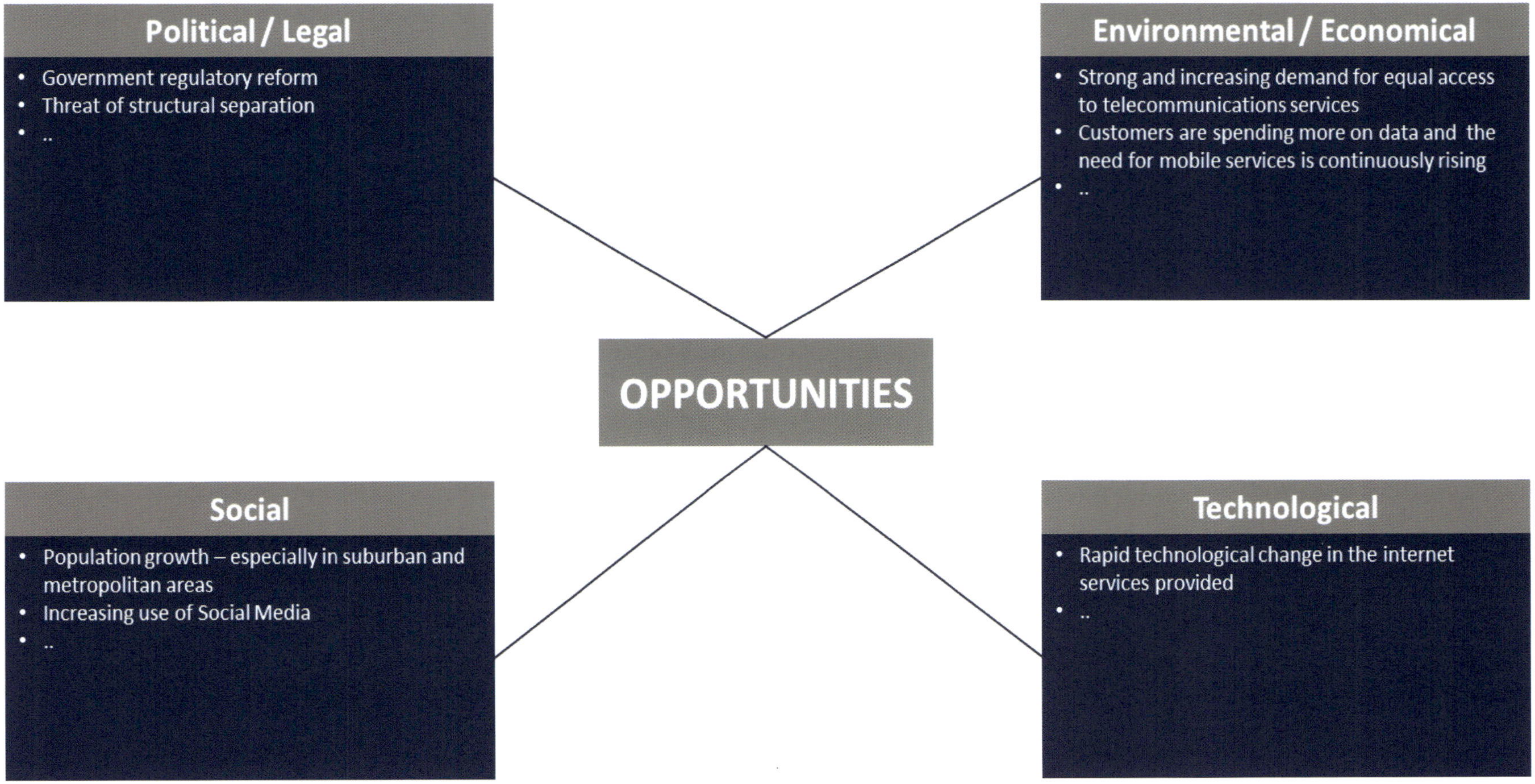

Political / Legal
- Government regulatory reform
- Threat of structural separation
- ..

Environmental / Economical
- Strong and increasing demand for equal access to telecommunications services
- Customers are spending more on data and the need for mobile services is continuously rising
- ..

OPPORTUNITIES

Social
- Population growth – especially in suburban and metropolitan areas
- Increasing use of Social Media
- ..

Technological
- Rapid technological change in the internet services provided
- ..

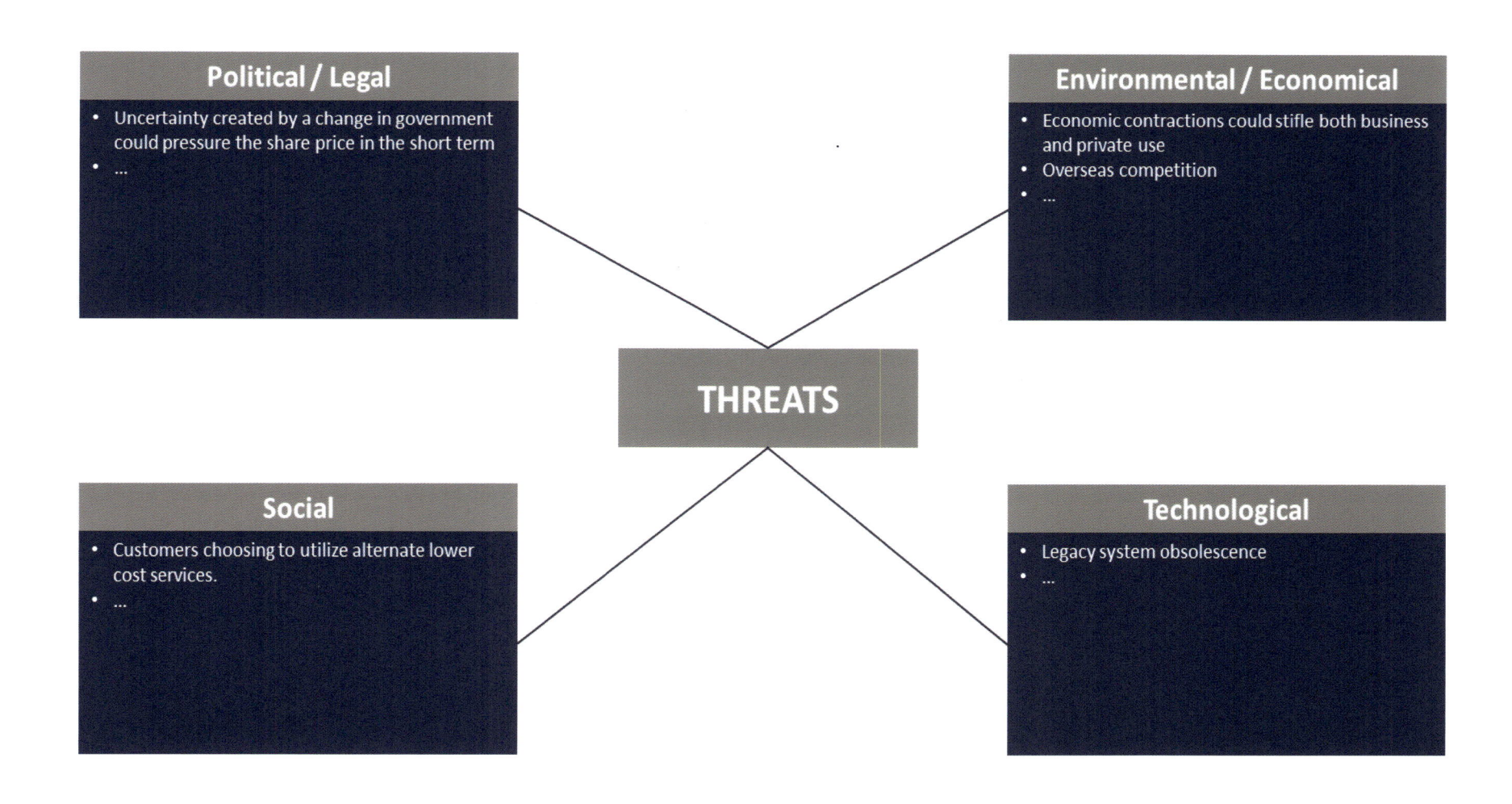

PEST Analysis Example – Opportunities

Political / Legal
- Uncertainty created by a change in government could pressure the share price in the short term
- …

Environmental / Economical
- Economic contractions could stifle both business and private use
- Overseas competition
- …

THREATS

Social
- Customers choosing to utilize alternate lower cost services.
- …

Technological
- Legacy system obsolescence
- …

Porter's Five Forces Analysis Example

Threat of New Entrants

- Low threat of potential entrants, as there are several barriers to entry – including market size, geography and capital requirements
- Even with capital, difficult to obtain and maintain brand reputation with such strong competition
- ...

Bargaining Power of Suppliers

- High supplier power due to limited supplier options
- ...

Rivalry Among Existing Competitors

- Expect the competitive intensity to increase as competitors improve network and restore brand
- Expect that competition will shift from aggressive platform-wide pricing adjustments to a generally more stable pricing environment.

Bargaining Power of Customers

- High switching costs
- Some customers have a high degree of dependency upon existing channels of distribution.
- Low bargaining power of customers

Threat of Substitutes

- Substitution risk has been recognized and pricing plans are being constructed to mitigate it.

Trend Summary Matrix

#	Key Market Trends	Evidence or Observation of Trends	Implications - Opportunities	Implications - Threats	Strategic Hypotheses	Competitive Advantage Gained?
1.	Customers have decreasing loyalty towards mobile phone operators.	Historically high churn rates and low customer satisfaction scores.	Competitor customers are potentially easier to lure away.	Inability to retain customers for extended periods of time – resulting in higher acquisition costs and reducing customer value and margins.	Operators needs to explore product and service differentiators that will provide the anchor to keep customers retained. Operators need to target service delivery improvements to lift customer satisfaction scores to increase loyalty.	Market differentiation and customer service improvement will provide a significant competitive advantage.
2.						
3.						

Mastering SWOT Analysis

Gain insight into an organization's competitive positioning through the tried-and-tested SWOT Analysis Method

> *I have been up against tough competition all my life. I wouldn't know how to get along without it.*
>
> — Walt Disney

Objectives of this Expert Toolkit Guide

1. Introduce the SWOT Analysis Method and outline how it adds value in a business context

2. Explain the 5-step process for conducting a SWOT analysis

3. Outline how to utilize the SWOT Analysis Method to develop strategic hypotheses

4. Share tips, lessons learned and limitations to be aware of when conducting SWOT analysis

5. Explain how the Strategic SWOT Method relates to the more comprehensive typical SWOT Analysis Method

An introduction to Porter's five forces

- SWOT analysis is a situational analysis of an organization's internal strengths and weaknesses and its external opportunities and threats.

- Strengths and Weaknesses are:
  - Characteristics of an enterprise across core dimensions such as people, process, technology, operations, assets and market position
  - Tangible assets including physical infrastructure, intellectual property, human capital and financial assets.

- Opportunities and Threats are:
  - Possibilities, constraints and other factors that can enable or impede the ability of an organization operating in a given market to achieve its objectives
  - External, environmental factors that can have positive or negative effects for a company operating within a given market environment

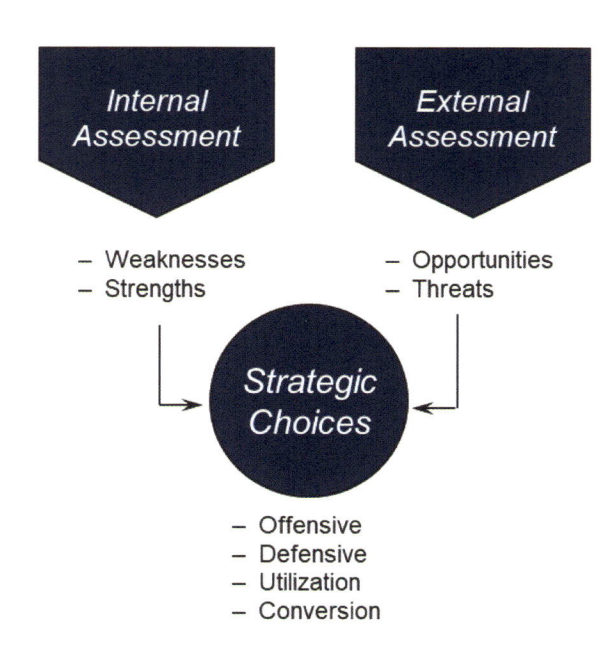

Internal Assessment
- Weaknesses
- Strengths

External Assessment
- Opportunities
- Threats

Strategic Choices
- Offensive
- Defensive
- Utilization
- Conversion

Combining the analysis of both internal and external strengths and weaknesses allows an organization to identify and assess strategic choices

SWOT analysis involves a 5 step process

The steps involved in SWOT analysis

1. Scope	2. Trends	3. External	4. Internal	5. Strategize
Determine the level and scope of the SWOT analysis	Identify market, competitor and environmental trends	Identify external opportunities and threats	Identify internal strengths and weaknesses	Develop strategic choices

These steps are related through an integrated framework

SWOT Analysis Framework

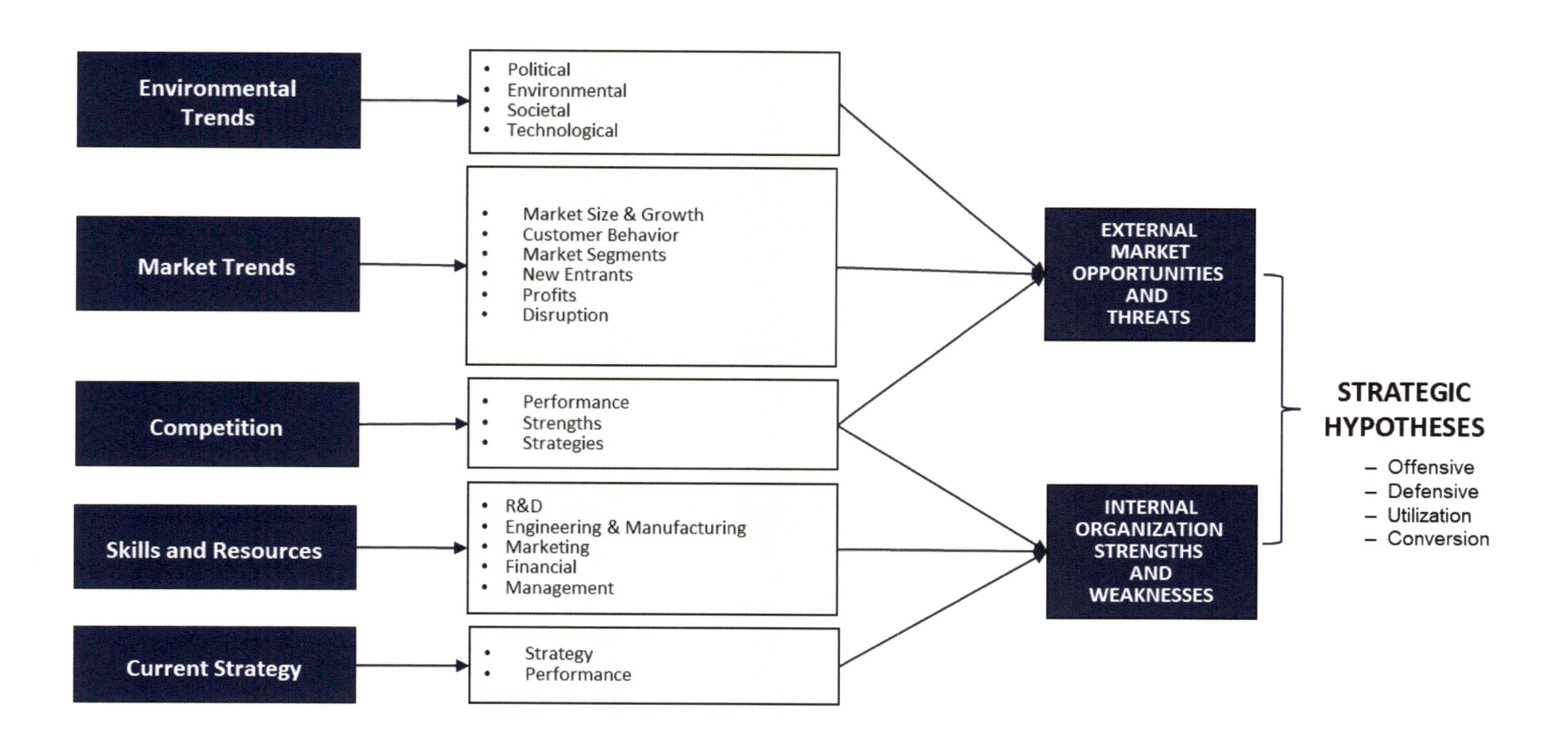

Input	Factors	Output	Result
Environmental Trends	• Political • Environmental • Societal • Technological	**EXTERNAL MARKET OPPORTUNITIES AND THREATS**	**STRATEGIC HYPOTHESES** – Offensive – Defensive – Utilization – Conversion
Market Trends	• Market Size & Growth • Customer Behavior • Market Segments • New Entrants • Profits • Disruption		
Competition	• Performance • Strengths • Strategies	**INTERNAL ORGANIZATION STRENGTHS AND WEAKNESSES**	
Skills and Resources	• R&D • Engineering & Manufacturing • Marketing • Financial • Management		
Current Strategy	• Strategy • Performance		

Step 1: Define scope of the SWOT analysis

Determine the Level and Scope of the SWOT Analysis

- Before commencing the SWOT Analysis, agree upon the level of detail required and the form of end deliverable desired. Be sure to clarify:

  - If the outcome of the analysis needs to be a text-based (high level) summary or a quantitative analysis including dimensions such as market growth and competitor costs?

  - It's critical to have this level of clarification to ensure that data collection is structured correctly, the right resources and time are allocated and to avoid any unnecessary work.

- The scope of the exercise should also be clearly determined to ensure that data collection and analysis is targeted and sufficient:

  - To focus the analysis, markets of interest should be defined and boundaries should be set for those markets.

  - Identify the primary competitors within each of the agreed markets.

  - Generally speaking, the span of the markets and competitors to be analyzed will be defined by the time, resources and skills that are available to perform the analysis.

Expert Tip!
Be conscious of the time and resources available to perform the analysis – this will heavily influence the level of detail that can be produced.

Expert Tip!
Text-based trend summaries are the easiest to do, quantitative analyses are the most difficult.

A clear scope is the foundation for a high quality SWOT analysis

Step 2: Identify the key trends

Identify Market, Competitor and Environmental Trends

- Performing an external trend analysis allows the identification of market, competitor and environmental trends.

- To perform external trend analysis, be sure to utilize existing organizational thinking and insights as a starting point to identify trends.

- Verification of trends is a critical aspect of this stage. Data for verifying trends should come from both internal and external sources:

  - Internal sources can include: executive interviews, employee interviews (e.g. marketing, sales, engineering), data from company systems (e.g. CRM, finance, order management).

  - External sources can include interviews with industry experts (e.g. industry analysts, trade associations), government bodies, regulators and advisory firms.

  - Don't overlook the personal and professional networks of team members performing the SWOT analysis when seeking sources to identify and confirm market trends.

Expert Tip!
Consult widely, look for diversity in your sources but be sure to confirm and "triangulate" information received.

Data sources should be identified in step 1 as part of a good data collection plan

Step 2: Identify the key trends

Market Trend Analysis Helps Identify External Opportunities

- It is important to understand the key trends that are relevant to the industry that is be analyzed. Isolate the trends that are most relevant to the industry or market segment being assessed.

- Trends can include items such as the following:

  — Size and growth rate of the market

  — Regulatory factors

  — Cyclicality

  — Seasonality

  — Segmentation

  — Product differentiation

  — Price sensitivity

  — Globalization

  — Customer needs & behaviors

  — Availability of substitutes

  — New entrants

  — Barriers to entry and exit

  — Supplier relationships

  — Profitability

Expert Tip!
Don't try and exhaust the possible list of trends. Gather a long list and consult with a variety of sources to arrive at a focused set of market trends.

Expert Tip!
Watch out for geography-specific or market-specific trends – verify trends utilized are relevant to the market / country / industry being analysed.

Step 2: Identify the key trends

Competitor Trend Analysis Helps To Pinpoint External Threats

- It is essential to understand the competitive landscape of the market. Identify the number, size, consolidation, vertical integration of competitors in the market that is being analyzed.

- For each competitor in the market, look across the key performance characteristics:
  - Investment in technology and innovation
  - Utilization of existing capacity
  - Cost structure
  - Market Strategy (e.g. Low cost versus premium provider)
  - Alliances and partnerships

- Like market trend analysis, focus the analysis on a limited number of competitors to ensure that the right level of detail can be reached with the time and resources available:
  - Keep the analysis targeted at relevant competitors
  - Cluster the competitors into groups – with the analysis focusing on a single competitor that is representative of each cluster.

Expert Tip!
"Relevant" competitors should be identified by market share, growth rate, profitability, degree of vertical integration or cost structure. Identify a representative sample of competitors with differing strategies and performance to understand reasons for strength or weakness.

Step 2: Identify the key trends

Use PEST Analysis to Identify Additional Opportunities and Threats

- PEST Analysis is a relatively straight-forward, but powerful method for identifying additional market factors that need to be considered.

  - **Political**

    - Indicates the likely impact of a government body or institution.

    - Includes regulation, taxation, monetary policy, tariffs, country-specific law, environmental law, trade rules.

  - **Economic**

    - Broad indicators of economic health.

    - Includes GDP, growth, unemployment, consumer confidence, inflation, interest rates, productivity, skills.

  - **Social**

    - Reflects cultural, societal and demographic influences on the market.

    - These include consumer behavior, age, income levels, education, purchasing power, preferences.

  - **Technological**

    - Includes innovations that impact products in addition to production processes.

    - Includes innovations in software, hardware, network technology, information flow, manufacturing processes.

Expert Tip!
Be sure to utilize all available sources of data, including: competitor analysis sources, existing market research, market research firms, interviews with market experts and database searches.

Expert Tip!
Use Expert Toolkit's Guide to PEST Analysis which can be found on experttoolkit.com

Step 3: Identify external opportunities and threats

Creating a Trend-Summary Matrix

- External opportunities and threats are evaluated in the SWOT Analysis approach by combining market, competitor and environmental trends in Trend-Summary Matrix.

- A Trend Summary Matrix provides a structure for summarizing trends and performing a trend analysis:

  - Capture the key trends

  - Provide evidence for each trend

  - Assess the implications (positive and negative) for the company

  - Identify the strategic options or hypotheses the are presented as a result of the trend and the implications

  - Consider if the strategic hypotheses will provide a competitive advantage or simply maintaining the status quo.

Trend Summary Matrix

#	Key Market Trends	Evidence or Observation of Trends	Implications		Strategic Hypotheses	Competitive Advantage Gained?
			Opportunities	Threats		
2.						
3.						
4.						

A Trend Summary Matrix template is presented on the next page

Step 3: Identify external opportunities and threats

A Trend Summary Matrix Translates Trends Through to Strategic Choices

#	Key Market Trends	Evidence or Observation of Trends	Implications		Strategic Hypotheses	Competitive Advantage Gained?
			Opportunities	Threats		
1.						
2.						
3.						
4.						

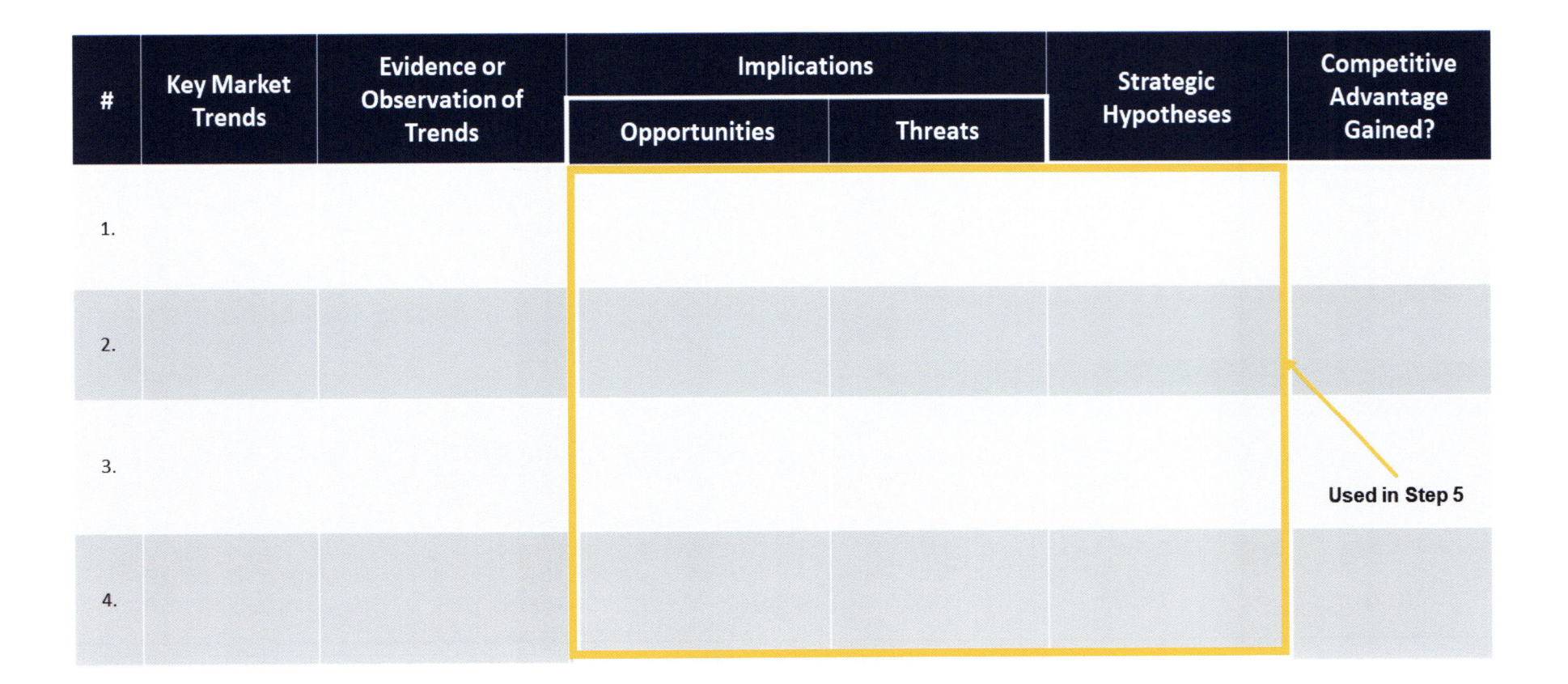

Used in Step 5

Step 4: Identify internal strengths and weaknesses

Assessing Strengths and Weaknesses Informs the Ability to Exploit Trends

- Using a variety of information sources, develop an initial view of the organization's strengths and weaknesses:
  - This can be developed through focused interviews, workshops, brainstorming sessions and data collection.
  - Use this information to create an initial long-list of strengths and weaknesses.

- Secondly, identify critical success factors related to each market trend:
  - These factors are what an organization needs to have in order to exploit a trend.
  - These factors can be found by looking at commonalities across successful competitors already in the market or market segment.
  - If the market is new and there are no existing competitors, brainstorm potential critical success factors based on expected customer needs.

Expert Tip!
Analysis effort should be spread across the organization and utilize a variety of information sources (qualitative and quantitative) to arrive at an objective and balanced view of the organization's true strengths and weaknesses.

Step 4: Identify internal strengths and weaknesses

Example Critical Success Factors

Marketing	Operations	Finance	Overall
Product: • Brand image • Product image • Breadth and depth of product line **Distribution:** • Network size, quality and strength • Channel coverage • Channel quality • Channel relationship strength **Marketing and Sales:** • Salesforce strength • Market power and skills • Market research and analytics • Salesforce quality	**Operations:** • Manufacturing cost • Technological advancement • Flexibility • Unique IP • Operational cost • Quality control • Locations • Unionization • Scale • Degree of vertical integration **Research and Engineering:** • Patents and IP • Product development skills and process excellence • Research skills, investment and capacity • Research partnerships	**Financials:** • Cash flow • Borrowing capacity • Equity • Capital • Credit • Bad Debt **Costs:** • Taxes • Cost base • Staff costs • Attrition	**Organization:** • Strategy • Vision • Structure • Culture • Values • Cross-organization collaboration **Management:** • Board strength • SLT strength

Step 4: Identify internal strengths and weaknesses

Evaluate Performance on Each Critical Success Factor

- Use the critical success factors in conjunction with the previously identified strengths and weaknesses long-list to create a prioritized short-list of dimensions to be assessed. This short-list should be those most relevant to the identified trends.

- Assess organizational performance by rating the company relative to each competitor across the consolidated list of dimensions:

    - Create a matrix with key dimensions on the vertical axis and competitors on the horizontal axis.

    - Utilize a simple rating scheme such as stronger, weaker, same/similar to rate the company against each competitor.

    - The level of precision and detail applied to performing this part of the analysis will largely be determined by time, resources and information available.

    - An example assessment matrix is show on the next page.

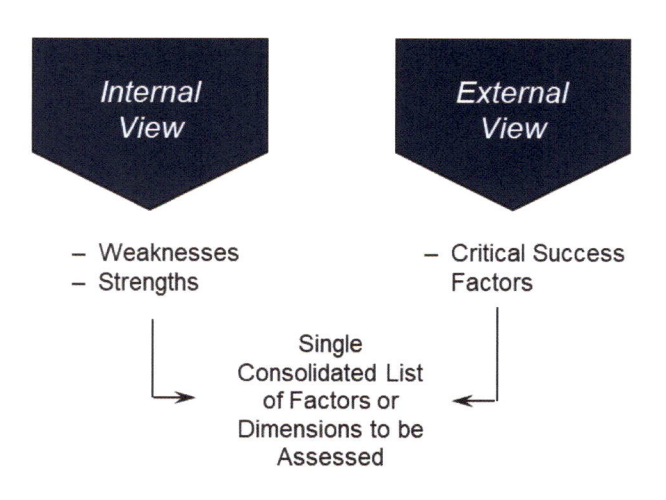

Internal View
- Weaknesses
- Strengths

External View
- Critical Success Factors

→ Single Consolidated List of Factors or Dimensions to be Assessed ←

Step 4: Identify internal strengths and weaknesses

Rate Performance Against the Competition

Key Dimensions	Competitor A	Competitor B	Competitor C	Competitor D	Overall Rating
Product Image	Stronger	Same	Stronger	Weaker	**Strength**
Retail Network	Stronger	Weaker	Stronger	Stronger	**Strength**
Distribution Network	Stronger	Same	Same	Stronger	**Neutral**
Marketing Skills	Stronger	Same	Stronger	Weaker	**Strength**
Manufacturing Costs	Weaker	Stronger	Stronger	Same	**Weakness**
Innovative Technology	Weaker	Same	Same	Same	**Weakness**
Unique IP	Weaker	Weaker	Weaker	Stronger	**Weakness**
Degree of Vertical Integration	Same	Weaker	Weaker	Weaker	**Weakness**
Research Skills	Stronger	Stronger	Same	Same	**Stronger**
Access to Capital	Weaker	Stronger	Same	Same	**Neutral**
Management Skills	Same	Stronger	Same	Stronger	**Strength**
Organizational Talent	Same	Stronger	Same	Stronger	**Strength**
Organizational Structure	Same	Stronger	Same	Same	**Strength**

A simple numbering scheme could also be utilized (1-5) to assess each competitor across the key dimensions – to provide a slightly more quantitative assessment.

Step 5: Develop strategic choices

The Results of SWOT Analysis Should Lead to Strategic Choices

- The final step brings it all together to develop strategic choices for the how the company can respond.

- This step involves combining:
  - The Opportunities, Threats and hypotheses identified in Step 3;
  - The Dimensions and Performance Assessment identified in Step 4.

- The recommended way to conduct this process is to develop a matrix with:
  - Key dimensions and company performance assessment from Step 4 on the vertical axis
  - Hypotheses developed in step 3 on the horizontal axis
  - The key dimensions listed in matrix should noted with "increase" if they increase the attractiveness of market opportunity or help to mitigate market threat.
  - The weaknesses should be marked with "decrease" if they decrease attractiveness of market opportunity or contribute to market threat.
  - Count the number of entries across the rows to identify strengths and weaknesses.
  - Add positive and negative entries in each column to identify opportunities and threats.

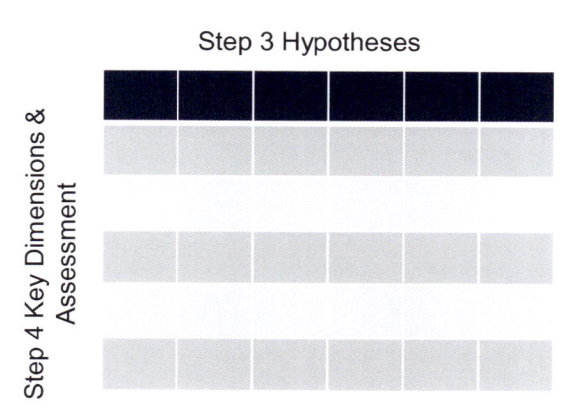

Step 5: Develop strategic choices

The Strategic Choices Development Matrix Leads to Specific Alternatives

A company's strategic focus should be set based on the opportunities and threats with the largest positive column sum in the Strategic Choices matrix. By summing the positive and negative entries, columns with largest positive values indicate the company has sufficient strengths to capitalize on opportunities and mitigate threats.

Key Dimensions	Opportunity A	Threat: Costs Not Competitive	Opportunity: Acquire New Customers	Threat: Competition Takes Customer	Opportunity: Product Enhancement	Threat: Over Engineered Product	Overall
Current Performance Rating - Strengths							
Product Image		Increase	Increase	Increase	Increase	Increase	2
Operational Scale			Increase				
Marketing Strength	Increase	Increase	Increase	Increase	Increase	Increase	6
Management Skills	Increase	Increase			Increase		3
Leadership	Increase	Increase					2
Corporate Structure	Increase						1
Current Performance Rating - Weaknesses							
Distribution Costs	Decrease	Decrease	Decrease	Decrease			-3
Technical Innovation	Decrease	Decrease	Decrease	Decrease			-3
Access to Capital		Decrease	Decrease	Decrease			-3
Degree of Vertical Integration	Decrease	Decrease	Decrease	Decrease			-3

The limitations of SWOT analysis

Although Effective, SWOT Analysis has challenges and limitations

- SWOT analysis provides a holistic, easily understood, easily utilized structure for the high-level analyses of businesses, markets and competition. It is a very useful method and tool for developing inputs that can be utilized in the development of a business strategy. These inputs can include feasibility assessments, critical success factor identification and option prioritization.

- However, before commencing a SWOT analysis exercise, it is important to be aware of the challenges and limitations that typically arise:
    - Specific market expertise or insight may be difficult to obtain or may be time consuming to gather
    - Not all market opportunities or threats might be identified
    - Important data can be difficult or time consuming to obtain
    - Quite often data that is obtained for the purposes of a SWOT exercise is in relatively raw form without indication of trends or insights
    - Data can also be subjective or difficult to quantify – particularly when obtained through interviews and not supported by quantitative data

Expert Tip!
When using SWOT analysis, it is important to identify secondary data sources that can be used for verification purposes

Mastering Competitor Analysis

Learn the method for assessing the competitive landscape and identifying offensive and defensive market opportunities

> "Competition is always a good thing. It forces us to do our best. A monopoly renders people complacent and satisfied with mediocrity."
>
> — Nancy Pearcey

Objectives of this Expert Toolkit Guide

1. Explain the purpose, principles and business insights that can be obtained through an effective competitor analysis

2. Describe the 7 step process involved in performing a competitor analysis

3. Provide expert tips to derive maximum value from a competitor analysis

4. Describe how competitor analysis can be used to inform the development of a business strategy

5. Equip you to be capable of performing a competitive analysis in a highly effective manner for maximum impact

An introduction to competition analysis

- Competitor analysis (or competition analysis) is an analytical method that seeks to compare organizations operating in the same market along a specific set of criteria

- The overall structure and format of competitor analysis will vary depending on the primary purpose and scope of the analysis but typically the following elements will be represented:

  - Competitor background including number of staff, geographic locations, leadership team, ownership structure & governance

  - Financial summary such as revenue, sales, margins, losses

  - Market positioning including market share, customer base

  - Product and service offerings

  - Strengths and weaknesses

  - Major announcements, acquisitions, divestures, partnerships and initiatives

Competitor analysis is performed to identify information that can be utilized for competitive advantage

Why we do competitor analysis?

The Purpose and Value of Competitor Analysis

- Competitor analysis is a proven method for assessing the competitive landscape in a given market and using the information to shape strategy. It is particularly helpful at answering several critical questions that inform business strategy, market development and execution:

  – Who is the competition? How many are there?

  – What are the characteristics and market positions of the competition?

  – What are the strengths and weaknesses of the competition?

  – How well are competitors performing and what are their strategies?

  – What market responses should expect to any moves that we make?

  – How is the competitive landscape changing?

  – Where do we have gaps in our offering, business model or capability set?

- Whilst not an end in itself, competitor analysis provides very useful insight and
direction for conducting further analysis. Competitor analysis is an efficient method for developing a view of competitors, their attributes and characteristics across a number of dimensions.

Expert Tip!
When performing competitor analysis don't neglect what might happen – don't assume competitors are standing still. Endeavor to explore their strategy and how their capabilities will evolve in the future.

Competitor analysis helps answer key questions

Questions Competitor Analysis Answers

1. Strengths
- What do we do better than our competitors?

2. Weaknesses
- What do our competitors do better than us?

3. Opportunities
- What products or services are currently not offered in the market and how can we take advantage of the situation?

4. Threats
- What are the risks we face in our business and how can we best address them?

These questions can be answered through analyzing competitors along several dimensions

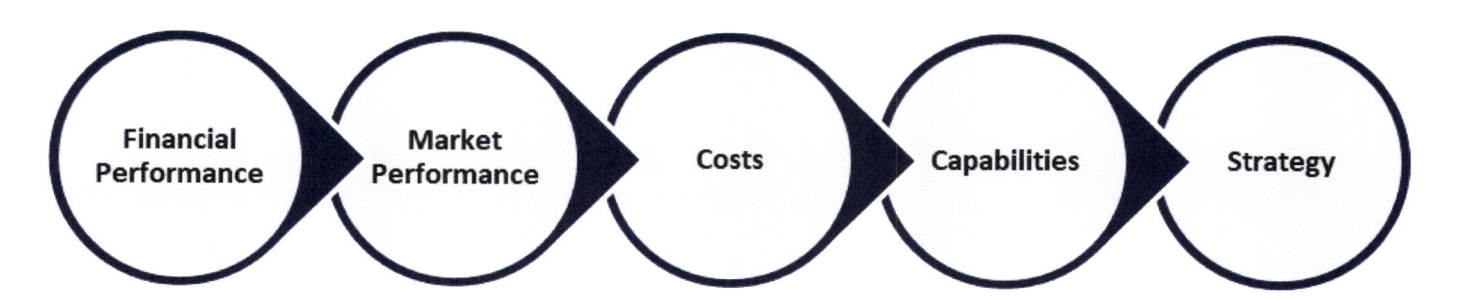

Financial Performance → Market Performance → Costs → Capabilities → Strategy

Competitor analysis involves 7 steps

Steps in Performing Competitor Analysis

1. Identify	2. Plan	3. Financial Assessment	4. Market Assessment	5. Cost Assessment	6. Capability Assessment	7. Strategy Assessment
Identify existing and potential competitors	Develop a plan for researching the competitors	Assess the financial performance of the competition	Assess the market performance of the competition	Assess the cost performance of the competition	Assess the capabilities of the competition	Assess the strategies of the competition

Step 1: Identify existing and potential competitors

Who Are Current Competitors and Those Who May Become Competitors?

Existing Competitors	Potential competitors
<ul><li>Companies that currently sell the same products and services in our market</li><li>Companies that currently sell products or services that address similar needs to ours</li><li>Companies that compete for limited space or time in the same distribution channels (e.g. shelf space, advertising space)</li><li>Companies that compete for the same customers mindshare, spend or recognition</li></ul>	<ul><li>Companies operating in other industries who could overcome entry barriers or exploit market changes</li><li>Companies who operating in the same industry but a different geography</li><li>Companies whose strategy could lead them to compete in your industry – especially as technology and other factors evolve</li><li>Companies who currently operate in a different position within the value chain – but could easily move to take a position in direct competition with your company</li></ul>

How do you identify existing and potential competitors?

- Interview Leaders
- Interview Sales Team
- Interview Customers

- Talk to Market Analysts
- Industry Specialists
- Industry Publications & Trade Journals

Step 2: Develop a research plan

A Clear Plan is Essential Before Performing a Competitor Analysis Exercise

- **Scope: Clearly understand and define the boundaries of the analysis**
  - Specify the markets, geographies, segments to be analyzed
  - Outline the structure and contents of the deliverable that needs to be produced

- **Purpose: Outline the overarching objectives of the competitor analysis exercise**
  - Clearly define the central objectives of the competitor analysis. Is it to understand a market before entering? Is it to inform strategic decisions regarding a customer segment, product offering or key competitor?

- **Time and Resources: Agree and allocate the necessary resources and time**
  - Agree the time available and any hard deadlines that need to be met
  - Identify the necessary skills and people available to perform the analysis
  - Specify the roles, accountabilities and responsibilities of the team
  - Layout the key activities, milestones, dependencies, inputs and outputs

- **Data Sources**
  - Agree the information that is going to be critical given the scope and purpose of the exercise
  - Identify the internal and external data sources that are available for intelligence gathering

Expert Tip!
Know your stakeholders – understand their expectations and critical requirements before proceeding with the competitor analysis exercise.

Expert Tip!
The key elements of the plan can be defined in a workshop with the team and critical stakeholders. This can save time and help avoid any misunderstandings.

Step 3: Assess financial performance

How Are Competitors Performing Across Standard Financial Metrics?

	Current Performance	Historical Performance	Financial Ratios*
Focus Area	• Standard financial measures – as absolutes and in percentage terms (e.g. of sales or assets)	• Rates of change in key financial measures over time	• Cost ratios • Margin ratios • Productivity ratios
Insight	• How the competitor is performing from an overall financial health standpoint and their relative position	• How financial health and relative position is changing over time	• Areas of significant difference which may reveal performance strengths or weaknesses

Expert Tip!
Financial performance analysis is a critical step and can reveal substantial insights influencing strategic decisions around customer segments, distribution, partnering, products, investments and areas requiring improvement.

Expert Tip!
Watch out for differences in treatment of gains and losses, one-off or extraordinary events, inflation, exposure to foreign exchange fluctuations.

Step 4: Assess market performance

How Are Competitors Operating And Performing In The Market?

	Market Share	Pricing & Value	Volume & Growth
Focus Area	• Market share across products and services within industries, geographies, segments, categories	• Current price and pricing approach and changes • Pricing inclusions, offers, value, discounts, terms	• Customer additions • Product volume • Customer losses (churn) • Units shipped
Insights	• How the competition is winning and capturing market share in specific areas	• How the competition is pricing to win and what customers are willing to pay and expecting to receive in value	• How the competition is performing on absolute volume measures and does this lead to more revenue and profit

Expert Tip!
Assess market performance on a "market by market" basis – which could be geographical, product or segment. Competitors may be winning in one market and losing in another market – it's important not to "average" performance across discrete markets as insights will be lost and findings misleading.

© 2019 Expert Toolkit | ALL RIGHTS RESERVED | USAGE PERMITTED AS PER USER AGREEMENT   The Strategic Advisor Expert Bundle   Page 142

Step 5: Assess cost (and profit) performance

How Are Competitors Managing Costs and Generating Profit?

- It's typical that competitors will have substantial differences in their cost base and associated profitability within specific customer segments or products and services.

- Individual market segments generally have varying costs-to-serve so it is important to assess product and service profitability at this level. Cost drivers for a specific product or service in a particular market segment can be derived by analyzing the value chain*.

- Two primary lenses can be applied when looking at profitability:
  - Product or Service Profitability
  - Customer or Segment Profitability

- Understanding product costs helps to make informed decisions such as: product pricing, portfolio rationalization or offer expansion. However, it is important to consider the stage of the product (or service) in the lifecycle – different cost and profit expectations exist depending on the stage of the lifecycle*.

Expert Tip!
Compare costs with direct competitors and other relevant companies such as those with similar issues or business needs.

Expert Tip!
Higher costs in an area does not always indicate under performance. It may result in greater value to the customer (and therefore higher prices and profits) or it may also be compensating for lower costs in another area. Be sure to look at the big picture before arriving at conclusions.

Profit = (Price - Variable Costs) x Volume - Fixed Costs

Step 5: Assess cost (and profit) performance

Analyze Costs Across Several Lenses

1. Financial Accounts

- Cost of Goods Sold (COGS)
- Employee Remuneration
- Interest Expenses
- Depreciation
- Taxes

2. Cost Accounts

- Direct Costs – Materials, Parts, Wages
- Overheads
- Indirect Costs
- Sales and Marketing Costs
- Administration Costs

3. Activity Based Costing (ABC)

- Sales Activities
- Operation Activities
- Marketing Activities
- Service Activities

4. Functional Accounts

- Marketing
- Production
- Operations
- R&D
- Finance

Expert Tip!

There is no "one size fits all" cost lens to apply. Consider the time and information available and leverage a mix of lenses to provide deeper insight. Financial and Cost Account information will be more readily available whereas ABC and Functional will be less available or require more time and effort to derive.

Step 5: Assess cost (and profit) performance

Examples of Cost Drivers

Manufacturing
- Number of products
- Number of staff
- Number of shifts
- Number of sites and distribution centers
- Number of outages or work stoppages
- Number of faults and quality errors
- Size of inventory – finished, raw and WIP

Telecommunications
- Number of retail stores
- Number of call centers
- Number of customer complaints
- Number of truck rolls
- Number of customer credits
- Number of distribution centers
- Number of customer calls
- Number of delinquent accounts
- Number of exchanges, points-of-presence or radio towers
- Number of faults
- Size of inventory

Banking
- Number of retail branches
- Number of call centers
- Number of accounts
- Customer acquisition costs
- Number of customer calls
- Number of delinquent customers
- Cost of capital
- Number of front-office staff
- Number of back-office staff
- Regulatory compliance costs

Where necessary talk to industry specialists to understand the specific cost drivers associated with an industry, market, geography

Step 6: Assess capabilities

What Are The Competitors' Capabilities?

- Capabilities are the underlying enablers an organization builds and utilizes to operate effectively in a given market and deliver value for their customers.

- Companies will often prioritize the capabilities for which they wish to be known as the "best" for and which they wish to heavily invest and improve. Correspondingly, companies may choose to de-prioritize capabilities they wish to just "keep up" or maintain.

- Examples of capabilities include customer service, network performance, brand, store presence, talent, systems, distribution, speed of delivery, operations excellence.

- There is a strong linkage between capabilities and overall business strategy. Understanding a competitors' strategy will indicate which capabilities they are likely to invest. Equally, understanding which capabilities a competitor is investing in will provide insights into their business strategy.

- Understanding the capabilities being prioritized by the competition can inform defensive positioning against the corresponding strategy and can inform the development of an offensive strategy in areas not being prioritized by the competition.

Step 6: Assess capabilities

Capability Categories

When considering the capabilities of the competition, take a broad perspective and be sure to assess the tangible and intangible. The map below provides a useful guide for capability areas to review.

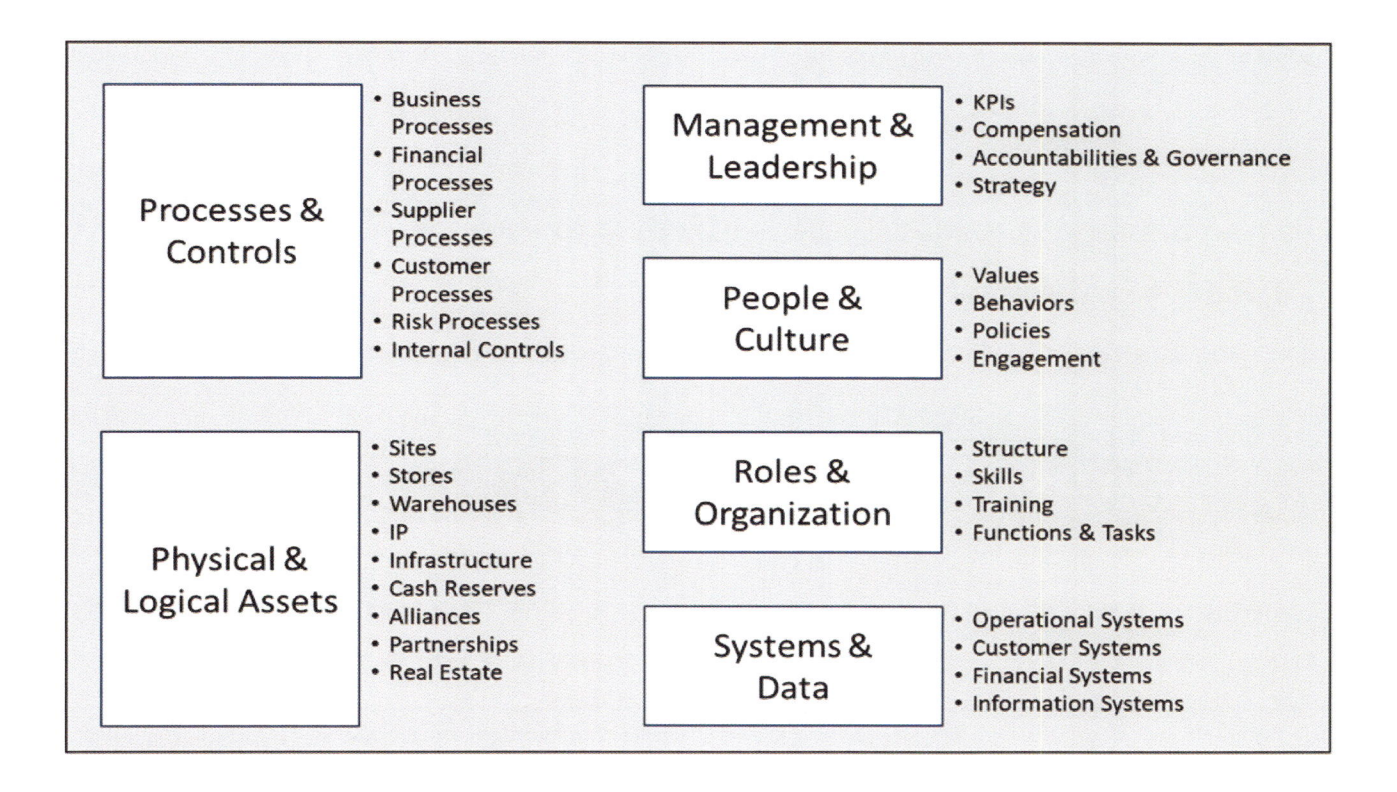

Processes & Controls
- Business Processes
- Financial Processes
- Supplier Processes
- Customer Processes
- Risk Processes
- Internal Controls

Physical & Logical Assets
- Sites
- Stores
- Warehouses
- IP
- Infrastructure
- Cash Reserves
- Alliances
- Partnerships
- Real Estate

Management & Leadership
- KPIs
- Compensation
- Accountabilities & Governance
- Strategy

People & Culture
- Values
- Behaviors
- Policies
- Engagement

Roles & Organization
- Structure
- Skills
- Training
- Functions & Tasks

Systems & Data
- Operational Systems
- Customer Systems
- Financial Systems
- Information Systems

Expert Tip!
Assessing capabilities can be as much art as science. Look at a variety of information sources to form a view and in particular talk to industry specialists and market analysts to understand their viewpoints on capabilities – always seek to get the "why" behind their views. Look for multiple data points to confirm viewpoints.

Step 6: Assess capabilities

Examples of Capabilities

Capabilities relevant to a competitor analyses will vary extensively by industry, geography and the purpose of the exercise. Be sure to focus on the capabilities most relevant to the analysis.

Capabilities	Description
Customer Acquisition	The ability to attract new customers
Customer Retention	The ability to defend existing customers against the competition
Service Recovery	The ability to rapidly remediate service delivery issues
Service Delivery	The ability to deliver quality service as expected by the customer
Customer Experience	The ability to provide a quality level of service and experience to the customer
Product Innovation	The ability to ideate, create and deliver new products and services to the market
Systems & Technology	The effectiveness and efficiency of underlying systems, platforms and applications
Workplace Culture	The ability to retain and motivate staff to perform at their best
Online & Digital	The ability to provide effective online channels for customers and partners
Access	The availability of stores, centers, sites for customers to connect, purchase, service
Agility	The ability of the company to adapt quickly to changing market conditions
Quality Control	The ability to produce high quality products with no defects

Step 6: Assess capabilities

Understanding Capability Positioning Informs Strategic Choices

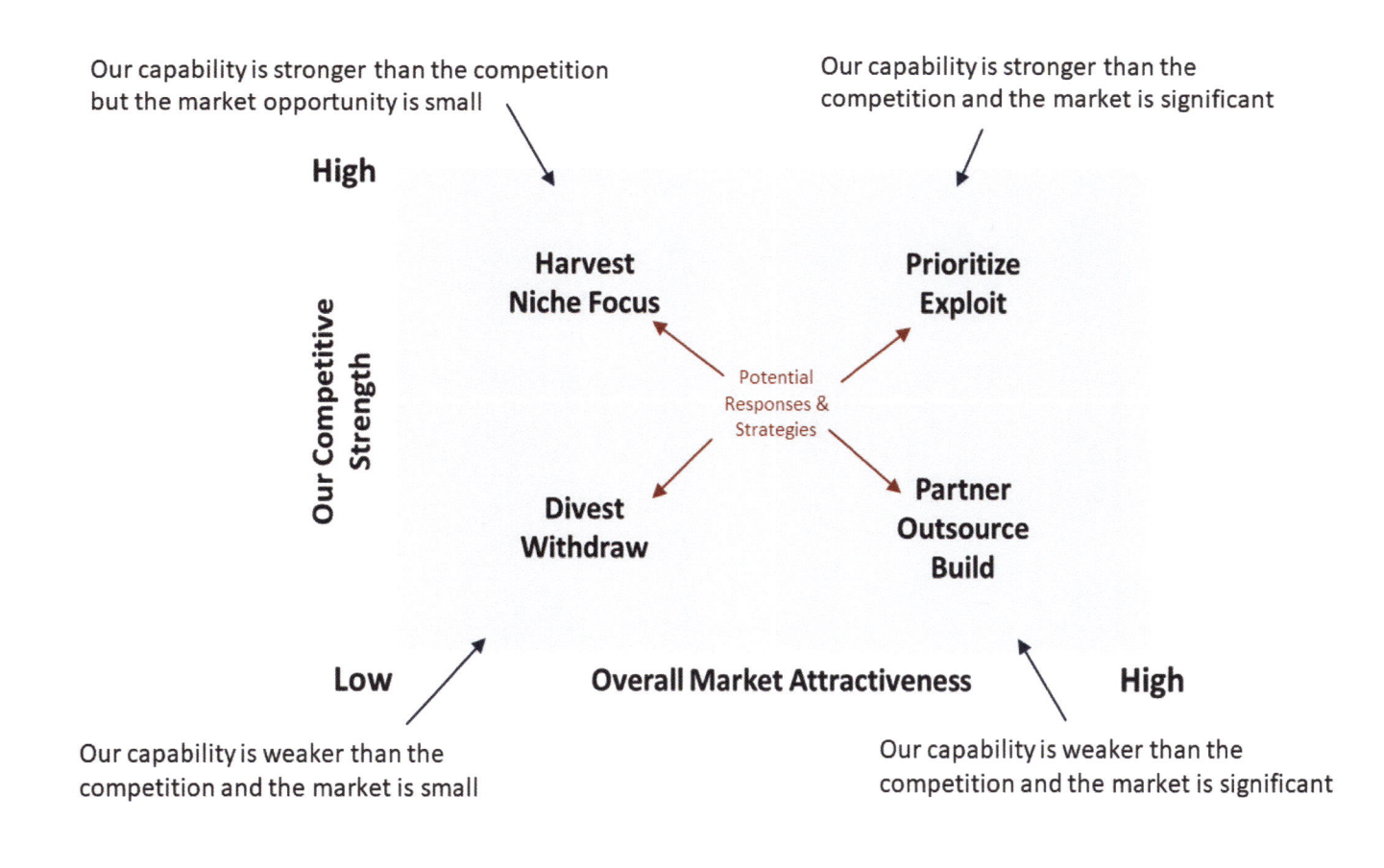

Our capability is stronger than the competition but the market opportunity is small

Our capability is stronger than the competition and the market is significant

High

Our Competitive Strength

- Harvest / Niche Focus
- Prioritize / Exploit
- Divest / Withdraw
- Partner / Outsource / Build

Potential Responses & Strategies

Low — Overall Market Attractiveness — **High**

Our capability is weaker than the competition and the market is small

Our capability is weaker than the competition and the market is significant

Expert Tip!
Consider the lifecycle or stage of development of a capability when informing strategic choices. For example, the capability may be early in its stage of development and maturity.

Expert Tip!
Consider the long term value of the capability – its relevance may be predicted to decline over time, or increase.

Step 7: Assess strategy

Where is the Competition Directing Their Priorities?

The final step in the 7 step process is the assessment of the strategies of the competition. This part of the analysis provides valuable forward-looking insight in the competition and where they are "placing their bets".

Focus Areas
- Marketing and branding
- Product launches or withdrawals
- Updates to offers and pricing
- Leadership changes and appointments
- Restructuring or reductions in staff
- Investments in real estate, warehouses, stores
- Major contract wins
- Partnerships, alliances, supplier appointments

Information Sources
- Publicly available information such as website, sales collateral, stock exchange or regulator submissions
- Public announcements and market announcements
- Industry specialists and market analysts
- Trade journals and industry publications

Potential Insights

- New product or service offering
- Entering or withdrawing from a market, geography or segment
- Major capability investments
- Competitor's views on the potential (or not) of a market segment or geography
- Restructuring to account for changes in the market dynamics, address performance issues or capitalize on a new market opportunity.
- Leadership changes to reposition the direction of the company or address internal execution challenges

Guide to Hypothesis-based Analysis

A powerful analytical technique to ensure business analysis is structured and focused on what matters

"Look and ye will find."

Unknown

Objectives of this Expert Toolkit Guide

1. Provide an overview of the hypothesis-based analytical approach and outline how it adds value in a business context

2. Explain the purpose and benefits of hypothesis-driven analysis

3. Outline the key steps involved in conducting hypothesis-based analysis

4. Describe the differences between good and bad hypotheses

5. Provide example of hypotheses

The 3 methods for conducting in-depth strategic or operational business analysis

Inductive and Abductive are alternates to Deductive reasoning

Traditional "Exhaustive" Bottom-Up Approach

Deduction → 1. Rule → 2. Case → 3. Result

Rule - If we put the price too high, sales will go down
Case - We have put prices too high
Result - Therefore, sales will go down

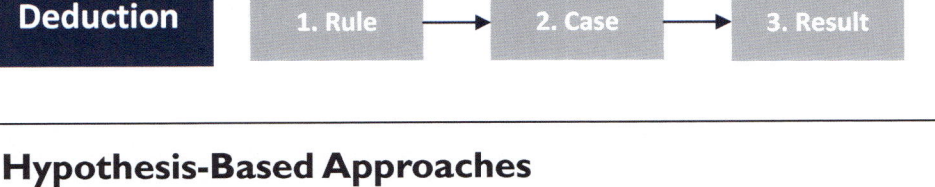

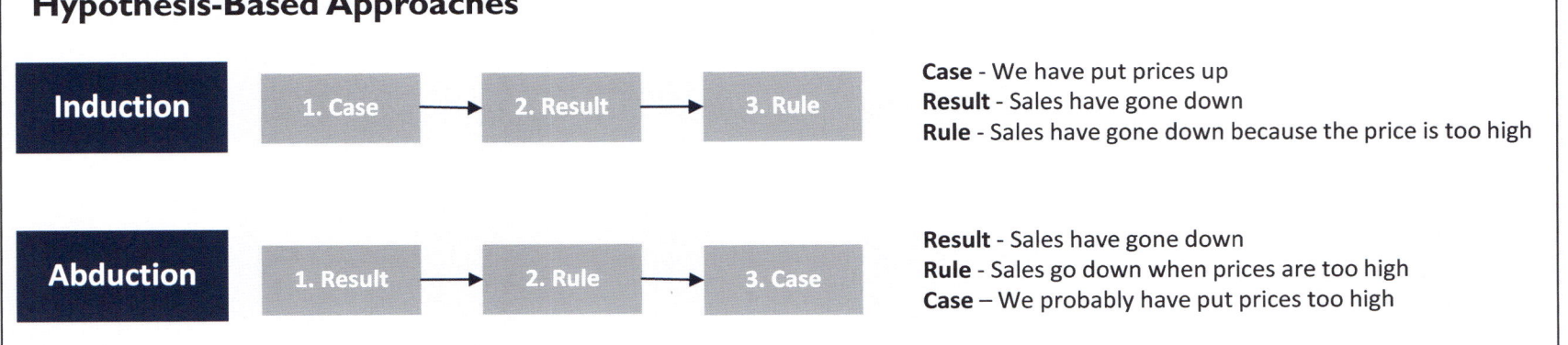

Hypothesis-Based Approaches

Induction → 1. Case → 2. Result → 3. Rule

Case - We have put prices up
Result - Sales have gone down
Rule - Sales have gone down because the price is too high

Abduction → 1. Result → 2. Rule → 3. Case

Result - Sales have gone down
Rule - Sales go down when prices are too high
Case – We probably have put prices too high

This Expert Toolkit Guide is primarily focused on the Inductive Hypothesis Method

Hypotheses help to ensure any analysis exercise is structured and focused

The 7 Steps to Building Hypotheses

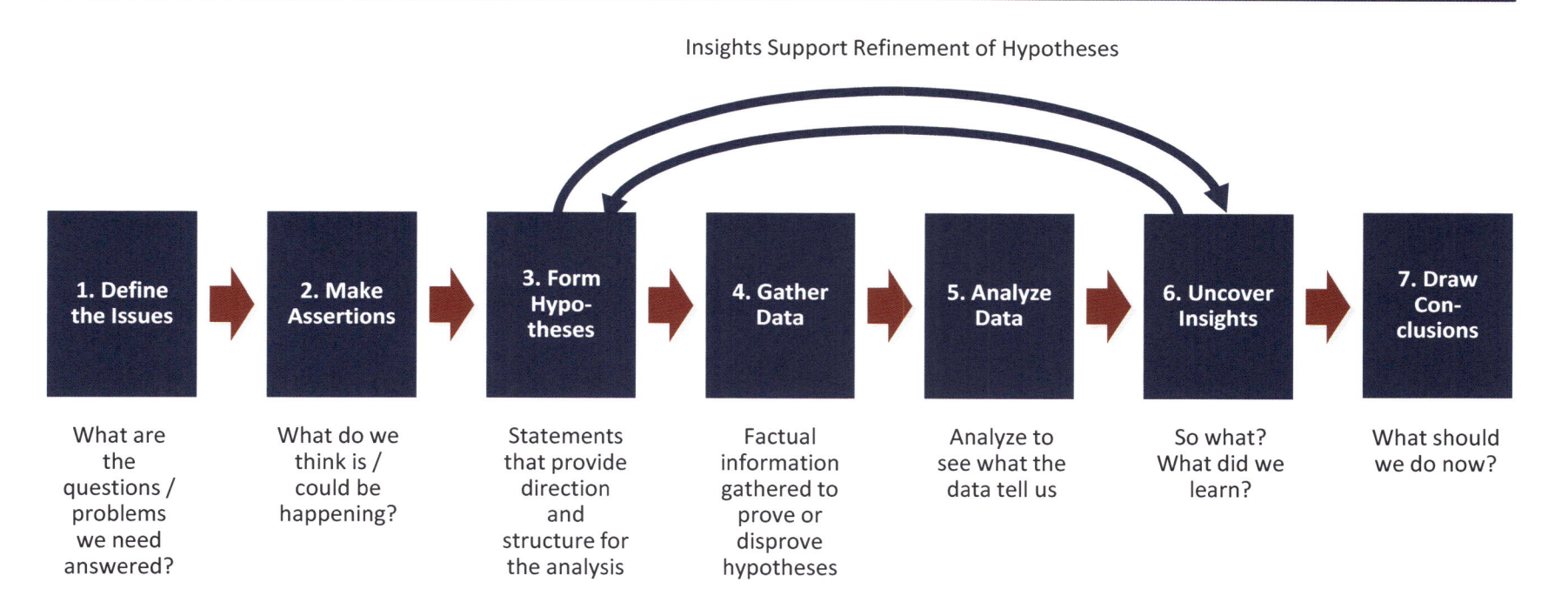

Insights Support Refinement of Hypotheses

1. Define the Issues	2. Make Assertions	3. Form Hypotheses	4. Gather Data	5. Analyze Data	6. Uncover Insights	7. Draw Conclusions
What are the questions / problems we need answered?	What do we think is / could be happening?	Statements that provide direction and structure for the analysis	Factual information gathered to prove or disprove hypotheses	Analyze to see what the data tell us	So what? What did we learn?	What should we do now?

Hypotheses provide a road map without which analysis could be directionless

Define question, review assertions, form hypotheses

Define the Question / Problem
- What are the real strategic issues / questions?
- What is the impact on the organization?
- What are the priorities?

Are we losing orders through poor quality sales processes?

Review and Describe Multiple Assertions
- We believe this to be true . . .
- A series of statements, not yet backed by data
- Based on initial data search or expert opinions

We believe that there might be fraud occurring on the front-line, which is causing the appearance of lost sales.

Form the Hypothesis
- We think . . .
- It looks like . . .
- The right answer may be . . .
- The options could be . . .

Absence of in-store controls are allowing sales orders to be manipulated, resulting in stock loss and no corresponding order.

A number of assertions need to be true for a hypotheses to be valid

Articulating a clear hypothesis helps determine the best analysis to be done

Hypotheses utilize "educated guesses" to accelerate identification of issues

Assertions:
- Stores are expensive
- Customers are willing to purchase products without entering a physical store
- Many retailers are successfully offering alternate channels (such as online)

↓

Hypothesis:
A retailer should close down half its stores and focus on alternate methods of sales and distribution

↓

Analysis:
- Customer analysis
- Financial analysis
- Industry analysis
- Competitor analysis

A hypothesis should identify not only the issue but also the likely cause and impact

Follow these steps as you create a hypothesis to help plan how to test it:

What is the issue?

– What is the underlying opportunity?

– Where is there an advantage to be gained?

"x is an opportunity ..."

What causes the issue?

– What are the key drivers of the process?

"...as a result of..."

What is the impact of the issue?

– How can we tell there is an opportunity?

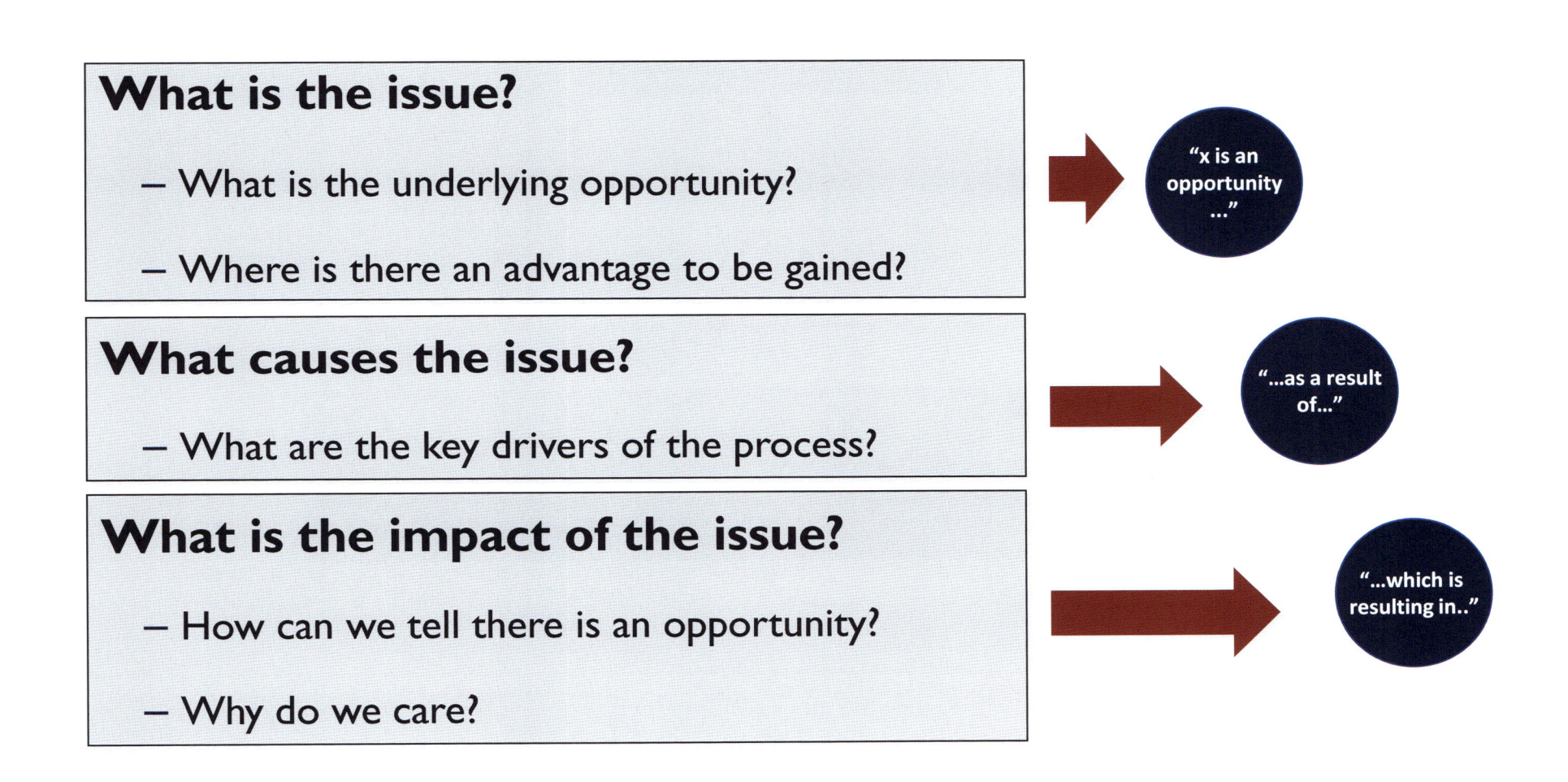

– Why do we care?

"...which is resulting in.."

Why are hypotheses valuable?

Key reasons why Hypotheses can be valuable

Focus — Hypotheses explicitly tie your analysis to a specific problem being addressed

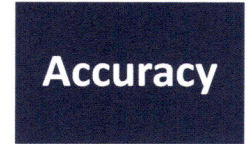

Accuracy — Hypotheses make it clear what level of accuracy is important

Efficiency — Hypotheses ensure analysis covers only the range needed to disprove hypotheses within a reasonable doubt

Action — Hypotheses allow a quick check before more extensive data collection and analysis is performed

Effectiveness — Hypotheses keep the work directed in areas of most value

What differentiates a good hypothesis from a bad one?

There are good hypotheses and there are bad hypotheses

Good Hypotheses	Bad Hypotheses
• **On Target**: Answer the core question being asked • **Accurate**: Encompass the range of competitive or profit drivers • **Supported by Assertions**: If true, then the hypothesis is correct • **MECE**: Mutually exclusive and collectively exhaustive • **Actionable**: Can be quantified and tested • **Affirmative**: Should be framed in the positive sense "this is happening", "we believe this to be true"	• **One-Sided:** Cannot be refuted • **Subjective:** Cannot possibly be quantified • **Too Vague or Broad**: Requires one to "boil the ocean" to verify • **Obvious:** Are so apparent or obvious that no one would logically, reasonably disagree with it • **Abstract:** Too theoretical, conceptual, impractical

Do your hypotheses meet any of the criteria on the right? Modify or drop them

How to develop high quality hypotheses

- There are proven generate high quality hypotheses:
  - Ask the front-line what they think is going on
  - Talk to industry subject matter experts
  - Talk to business and technical executives
  - Talk to people along the entire value chain
  - Have brainstorming sessions (use the Affinity Diagram approach)
  - Use the 5 Whys Approach
- Once you have initial hypotheses, validate them:
  - Look at any easily available data
  - Visit the "front-line" - watch and see if you can see what's going on
  - Validate them with people you have talked to

What if a hypothesis is proven wrong?

- Hypothesis-driven thinking requires frequent reviews of the prevailing and current hypotheses:

  - Do we still think they are correct?

  - Are we making progress towards disproving them?

  - Did we overlook some data or insights?

  - Are we making any poor assumptions?

  - Are they at the right level of detail?

- With all testing outcomes – when the answer is unexpected, it reveals something not known – that's a good thing.

- Having proven a hypothesis wrong means you have made a step towards answering the question and getting to the heart of the issue (something has been ruled out – perhaps a myth?).

Example Hypothesis Development and Capture Template

Problem / Question	Assertions	Hypotheses	Data Sources / Lines of Inquiry	Findings / Insights	Conclusions
Are we losing orders through poor quality sales processes? Sales orders and in-store stock are not reconciling.	There might be fraud occurring on the front-line, which is causing the appearance of lost sales. This is a common problem in this industry, and we have experienced it previously.	Absence of in-store controls are allowing sales orders to be manipulated resulting in stock loss and no corresponding order.	Order Data, Stock Data, Store Mystery Shopping, Store Observations	At stores X, Y and Z, stock levels and order levels are inconsistent by 3500 units (13%) for the month of April. We have a large number of orders being processed to dummy accounts with no customer attached. These orders are concentrated amongst a finite set of sales reps.	
Is our multi-channel sales and distribution model optimally design for customer experience and revenue?	Stores are expensive, customers are willing to purchase products without entering a physical store, and many retailers are successfully offering alternate channels (such as online).	We should close down approximately half of our stores and move an equivalent volume to online.	Financial data, Competitor benchmarks, Store traffic data, Online industry analysis, Customer purchasing research		

How to use to the Accelerated SWOT Method

A simple, but powerful method for thinking through your strategic initiatives taking into account market dynamics and your capabilities

> *In preparing for battle I have always found that plans are useless, but planning is indispensable.*
>
> — Dwight D. Eisenhower

Objectives of this Expert Toolkit Guide

1. Provide an introduction to the Accelerated SWOT Method

2. Outline the step-by-step approach for utilising the Accelerated SWOT Method

3. Provide an example to illustrate how the Accelerated SWOT Method works in practice

4. Provide Expert Tips for using the method effectively

The Accelerated SWOT Method

When to use it

- When you need to take a fresh perspective on market conditions and how they line up against corporate capabilities
- When you need to drive alignment across your team at the strategic level
- When you are looking for a simple and straightforward method to validate your strategic programs against and overarching corporate strategy
- When time or resources do not permit use of the more comprehensive SWOT analysis method

Problems it helps solve

- Lack of clarity on key strategic imperatives
- Lack of confidence that current strategic imperatives take into account current corporate strengths, weaknesses and market conditions
- Lack of strategic alignment across the leadership team
- Lack of creative thinking around strategic choices that are available to the organization

Introducing the accelerated SWOT method

What is the Accelerated SWOT Method

The Accelerated SWOT Method is a simple approach that matches corporate capabilities against market conditions in order to develop strategic choices. The technique uses a simple grid (as shown below) to present trends, strengths, weakness and strategic choices all on a single panel.

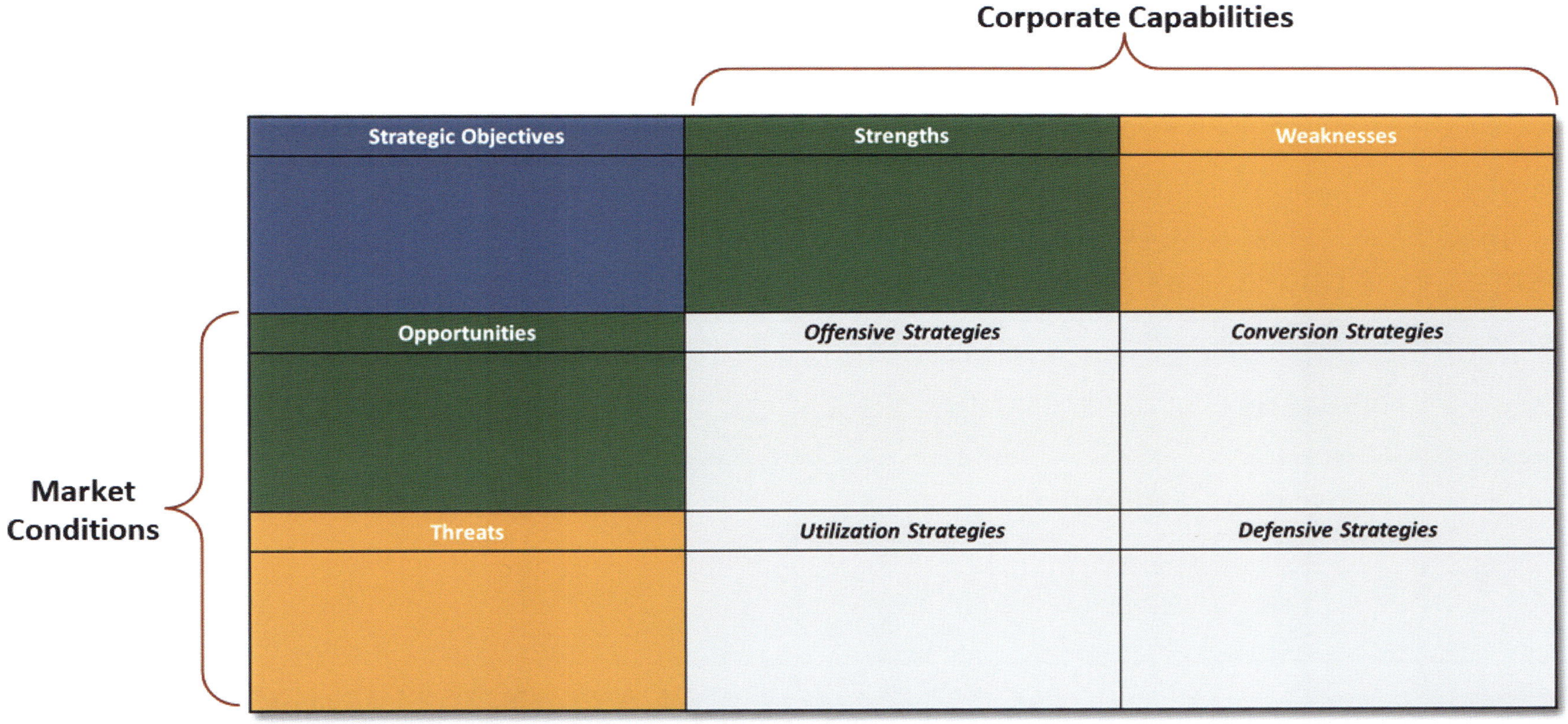

Corporate Capabilities

Strategic Objectives	Strengths	Weaknesses
Opportunities	*Offensive Strategies*	*Conversion Strategies*
Threats	*Utilization Strategies*	*Defensive Strategies*

Market Conditions

The accelerate SWOT method involves a 4 step process

The steps involved in accelerated SWOT

1. Objectives

Capture the corporate objectives

2. Market

Identify market, competitor and environmental trends, threats, opportunities.

3. Capabilities

Identify internal strengths and weaknesses

4. Strategies

Develop strategic hypotheses

Step 1: Capture corporate objectives

Identify and Document the Organization's Corporate Objectives

Using existing information and stakeholder interviews, document the organization's corporate objectives. If performing the accelerated SWOT on a subset of the organization, use those objectives (for example, business unit, geography, product line).

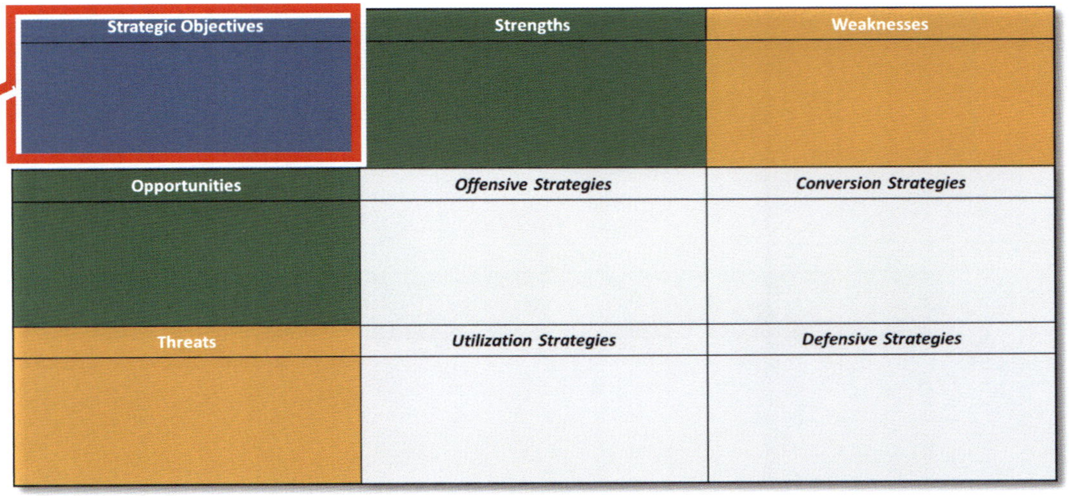

Strategic Objectives	Strengths	Weaknesses
Opportunities	*Offensive Strategies*	*Conversion Strategies*
Threats	*Utilization Strategies*	*Defensive Strategies*

Step 2: Market conditions

Identify and Document the Market Trends

Using existing information and stakeholder interviews, document the key trends that are relevant to the business unit, product, geography used in step 1. Focus on the most influential trends that create opportunities or threats. Trends are conditions that impact all organizations or products in the market and can include regulatory, economic, societal, technological.

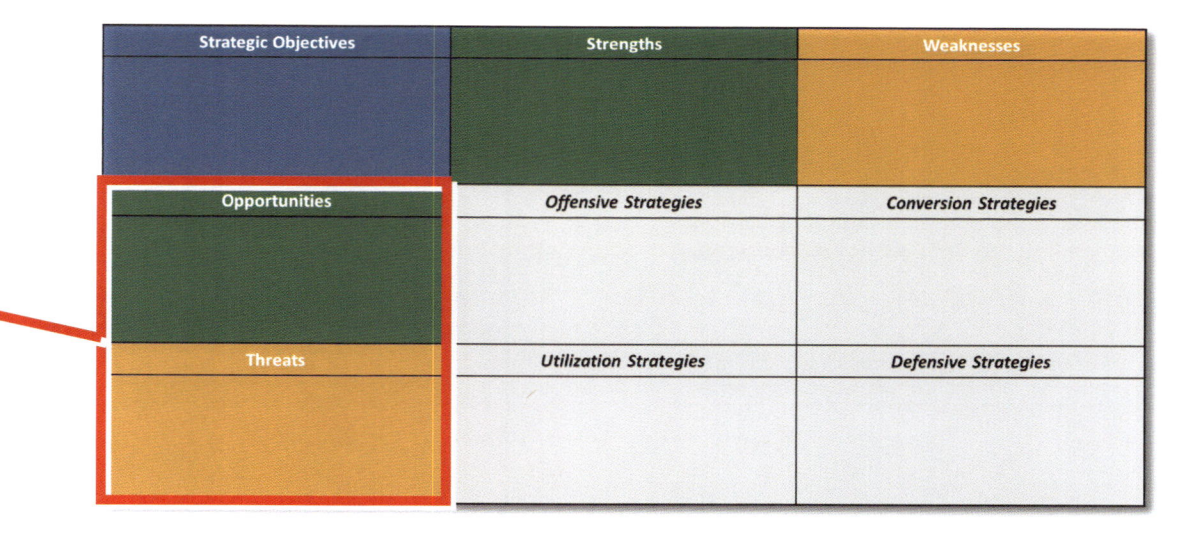

Strategic Objectives	Strengths	Weaknesses
Opportunities	Offensive Strategies	Conversion Strategies
Threats	Utilization Strategies	Defensive Strategies

Step 3: Assess capabilities

Identify and Document the Corporate Capabilities

Using existing information and stakeholder interviews, document the assessment of internal capabilities. Focus on the key capabilities that are seen as core strengths or weaknesses within the organization.

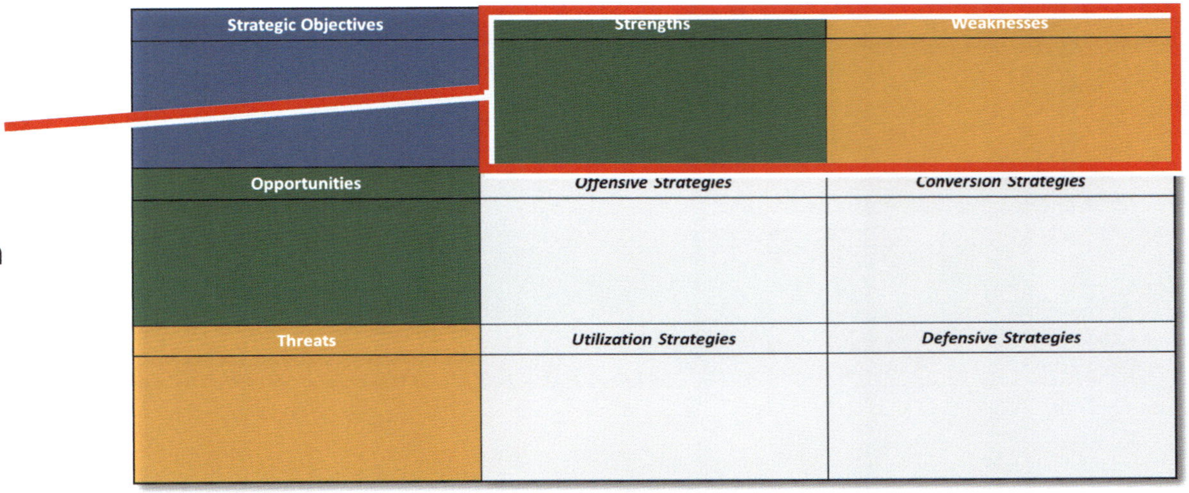

Strategic Objectives	Strengths	Weaknesses
Opportunities	Offensive Strategies	Conversion Strategies
Threats	Utilization Strategies	Defensive Strategies

Step 4: Develop strategies

Identify and Document the Corporate Capabilities

With an eye on the Strategic Objectives captured in the top left box, brainstorm potential strategic choices for the organization. Take on each section (Offensive, Conversion, Utilization, Defensive) sequentially.

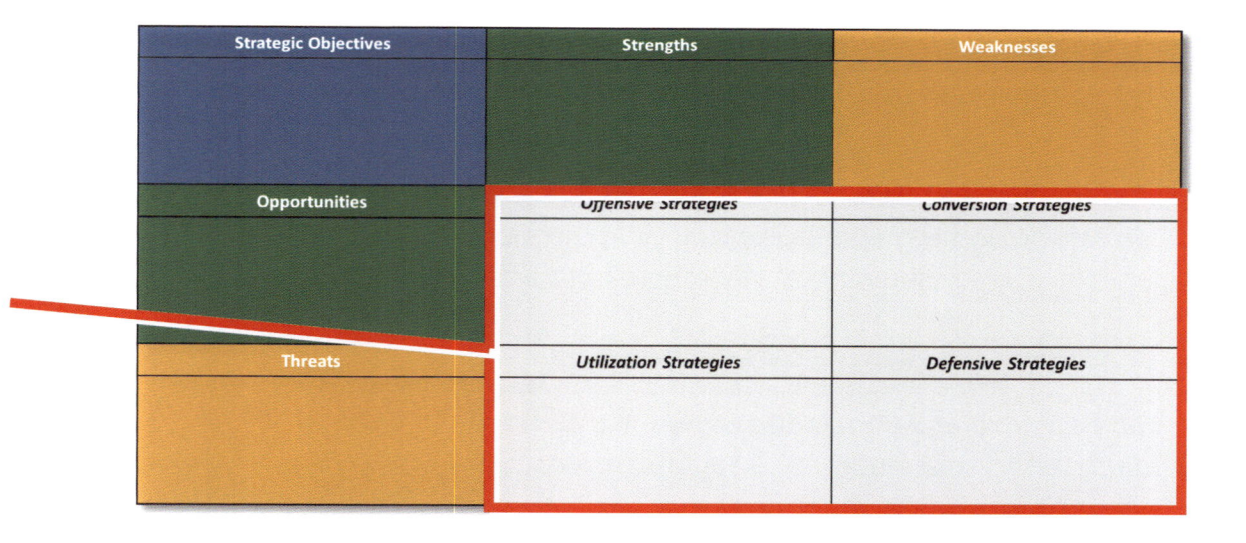

Strategic Objectives	Strengths	Weaknesses
Opportunities	Offensive Strategies	Conversion Strategies
Threats	Utilization Strategies	Defensive Strategies

Step 4: Develop strategies

The Four Strategies Explained

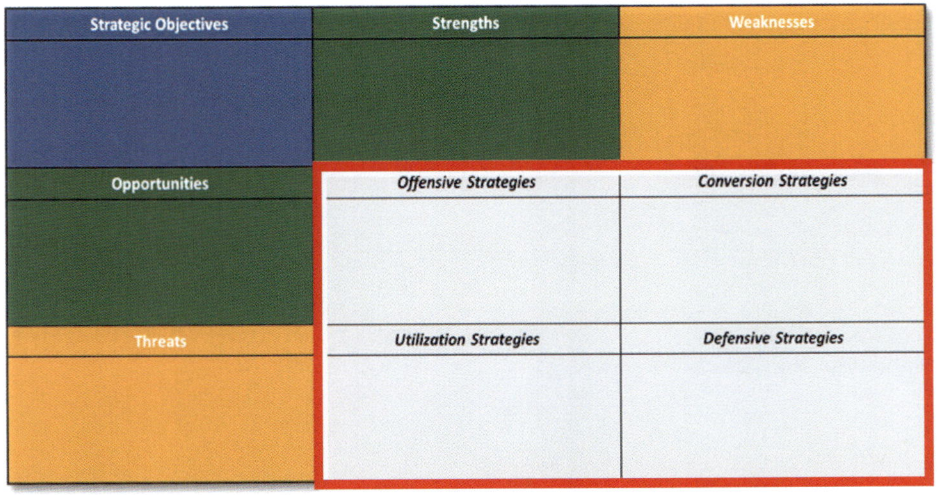

Strategic Objectives	Strengths	Weaknesses
Opportunities	Offensive Strategies	Conversion Strategies
Threats	Utilization Strategies	Defensive Strategies

Offensive Strategies = Strengths plus Opportunity. Where can a market opportunity be exploited by leveraging a corporate strength.

Conversion Strategies = Weakness plus Opportunity. Where can market opportunities be leveraged to overcome a corporate weakness.

Utilization Strategies = Strength plus Threat. Where can a Strength be leveraged to overcome a market threat.

Defensive Strategies = Weakness plus Threat. What strategy can be employed to neutralize a weakness at the same time as mitigating a threat.

An example accelerated SWOT grid

Strategic Objectives	Strengths	Weaknesses
1. Drive domestic market share 2. Improve customer service 3. Improve operating margins 4. Expand into Eastern Europe 5. Lift shareholder value	1. Premium brand 2. Strong balance sheet 3. Offshore distribution centers 4. Retail sales footprint 5. R&D Capability	1. High operating cost base 2. Poor sales processes 3. Complex legacy systems 4. Unionised workforce 5. Limited big deal experience
Opportunities	*Offensive Strategies*	*Conversion Strategies*
1. Eastern Europe Conditions 2. Potential for alliances 3. Technology increasing demand 4. Sustainability agenda	1. (S1+O1+O2) Distribution alliance with XYX in Romania leveraging our brand 2. 3.	1. (W2+O1) Complete a process re-engineering exercise to support efficiency + market expansion 2. 3.
Threats	*Utilization Strategies*	*Defensive Strategies*
1. Increasing competition 2. Pricing pressure 3. Increasing deal complexity 4. Suppliers competing 5. Cyber security risks	1. Leverage balance sheet to purchase #3 competitor (S2+T1) 2. 3.	1. Conduct a cost optimisation program to improve margins and prepare for increasing price pressure (W1+T1+T2) 2. 3.

Accelerated SWOT grid template

Strategic Objectives	Strengths	Weaknesses
Opportunities	*Offensive Strategies*	*Conversion Strategies*
Threats	*Utilization Strategies*	*Defensive Strategies*

Expert Tips using the accelerated SWOT method

- Be sure to complete the exercise in the order recommended on page 6
- Having a very clear view of your overarching Corporate Strategic Objectives is critical. If you don't have these – do not proceed any further!
- Strengths and Weaknesses apply to your organization
- Opportunities and Threats apply to the market (not just your organization). A good check is that each market opportunity or threat should equally apply to your competition
- Build the Accelerate SWOT grid in collaboration with your peers and leadership team. It is a great tool for gaining agreement on the critical capabilities, market conditions and strategic imperatives.
- Each of the Strategies should be specific enough to clearly articulate what needs to be done but not attempt to define exactly how it will be done. That comes next!
- Populating the Defensive Strategies section is generally the most difficult. Think:
- What strategies do we need to put in place to overcome critical weaknesses and counter a market threat

Notes

Notes

Notes

Notes

Notes

Disclaimer

- Descriptions and other related information in this document are provided only to illustrate the methods covered. You are fully responsible for the use of these methods where you see appropriate. Expert Toolkit assumes no responsibility for any losses incurred by you or third parties arising from the use of these methods or information.

- Expert Toolkit has used reasonable care in preparing the information included in this document, but Expert Toolkit does not warrant that such information is error free. Expert Toolkit assumes no liability whatsoever for any damages incurred by you resulting from errors in or omissions from the information included herein.

- Expert Toolkit does not assume any liability for infringement of patents, copyrights, or other intellectual property rights of third parties by or arising from the use of Expert Toolkit information described in this document. No license, express, implied or otherwise, is granted hereby under any patents, copyrights or other intellectual property rights of Expert Toolkit or others.

- This document may not be reproduced or duplicated in any form, in whole or in part, without prior written consent of Expert Toolkit.

- The document contains statements that are general in nature and do not constitute recommendations to the reader as to the content's suitability, applicability or appropriateness.

Printed in Poland
by Amazon Fulfillment
Poland Sp. z o.o., Wrocław